THE TEN SPEED
COMMANDMENTS

Also by Mike Keefe

RUNNING AWRY
KEEFE-KEBAB

The Ten Speed Commandments

AN IRREVERENT GUIDE TO THE COMPLETE SPORT OF CYCLING

MIKE KEEFE

A DOLPHIN BOOK
Doubleday & Company, Inc., Garden City, New York
1987

Library of Congress Cataloging-in-Publication Data

Keefe, Michael.
  The ten speed commandments.

  Bibliography: p. 131.
  1. Cycling—Anecdotes, facetiae, satire, etc.
I. Title.
PN6231.C92K4 1987   796.6'0207   86-29233
ISBN 0-385-23803-7

FOR BRADY JOSEPH KEEFE

ACKNOWLEDGMENTS

For help, support, suggestions, and patience, the author would like to thank, among others, Bill Wildberger, Susan Schwartz, Anita Austin, Delaney Keefe, Gary Reilly, Craig Carver, Fred Brown, Brandon Strong, and Claire Martin.

THE TEN SPEED COMMANDMENTS

INTRODUCTION

For some unfathomable reason, bicycle riding has become tremendously popular in recent years. Although this is purely conjecture, it probably has something to do with Steven Spielberg. Everything else does.

At last count 5,387,562,102 kids and regular-sized people confessed to having experimented with bikes on occasion, though few would admit to using them habitually. There are still a handful of humans left on earth who wouldn't know a bicycle from dental plaque. Most of these people live, naturally, in extremely isolated sections of the globe such as Friendly Bob's Mobile Home Park on the outskirts of Muncie, Indiana. Inevitably, though, they will also be consumed by the explosion of interest in cycling.

This book is designed to be an introduction and complete guide to a wonderful recreational machine. For the beginning cyclist, *The Ten Speed Commandments* is a handy reference with sections on commuting, touring, racing, bicycle selection, equipment, maintenance, and more. For the more advanced rider, this book can serve as a paperweight or kindling.

Read this book now. Learn all you can about the fascinating sport of bicycling while there's still time. This "bike boom" will last maybe three more months, tops.

How to Use this Book

Begin reading *The Ten Speed Commandments* on page one. When you have completed page one, find page two. Read page two. Continue reading the pages in sequential order until you have reached the end of the book.

How to use this book as a temporary bike rack.

Highlight important passages in the book with a yellow felt-tip marker. For example, vital information such as "Tanzania's leading export is tin" should be underlined, whereas a statement such as "Get in touch with your feelings" ought to be ignored since, as you know, it is absolutely devoid of meaning.

After you've finished this book, attach it to the handlebars of your bike. Questions will arise during a ride that can be answered quickly and conveniently by flipping to the appropriate paragraph. Avoid reading lengthy chapters in heavy traffic.

Questions most often asked by readers are addressed in the Letters section. Professor Ten-Speed, a noted cycling expert, romance novelist, and inventor of the digital kazoo, was recruited to field readers' inquiries. You will find his replies brief, informative, and at the back of the book.

When you have become completely familiar with your bicycle and thoroughly versed in cycling lore, you may use this book as a temporary bike rack.

Chapter 1

Bicycling for Exercise

Take a long, critical look at yourself. Now be honest. On a ten-point scale how would you rate yourself if Sylvester Stallone is a ten and Garfield is a zero? Note: this is a physical rating, not a mental one. If you find yourself on the lower end of the spectrum, you probably tire easily, eat too much, and require an elaborate arrangement of ropes and pulleys to remove yourself from the bathtub. This book was written especially for you.

It was also written for anybody else who can scrape together the cover price.

Riding a bicycle is the best way to get in shape. Running is okay but it gives you blood blisters and turns the cartilage in your knees to Malt-o-Meal. Also, as of this writing, the so-called "runner's high" is illegal in thirty-seven states and the District of Columbia. Aerobics classes are more like fashion shows than workouts. They are often nothing more than thinly disguised sexual displays in which perfectly proportioned young men and nubile twenty-five-year-old women, dressed in stretch garments approximately the thickness of an electron, throb and undulate to suggestive rock lyrics. Granted, it's a great spectator sport, but your concern is conditioning, not entertainment. Tennis and racquetball consist, primarily, of walking across a court and picking up a ball. Swimming is for fish.

Health Benefits

Bicycling builds bodies better than a *Playboy* airbrush artist. All muscle groups, bones, vital organs, and glands, with the exception of taste buds and those little hairs on the small of your back, benefit from a regular program of bicycle exercise. Let's be specific.

Cardiovascular Development

The cardiovascular system is something that appeared suddenly in man sometime in late 1972. Those billions of people who lived full lives prior to 1972 could drink and smoke and horse down Hostess Sno-balls without ill effect. Today, those same activities are immediately fatal. Doctors and scientists and people who write fad paperbacks have determined that a person must spend at least three hours a day sweating and breathing hard. Those who ignore the existence of their cardiovascular system quickly run out of small talk at parties and are forced to discuss the international banking crisis or Tolstoy.

Riding a bicycle is a highly recommended way to avoid profound conversation.

Muscle Tone

You might, at first, think that the only muscles conditioned by bicycling are your basic leg muscles. Wrong. Every single muscle you can name benefits from cycling. Go ahead, name one. The eyelid muscle? The eyelid muscle controls the squint response, which occurs when a blast of air threatens to dry your eyeball, causing it to make an unpleasant scratching sound when you look from side to side. Also, when a grain of road dust lodges behind your contact lens, the eyelids clamp shut on the theory that it's best to immobilize the injury to give the victim sufficient time for moaning and yowling. Both of these conditions are familiar to cyclists who regularly exceed twelve miles per hour. Would you like to name another muscle? No? Good, now we can go on.

The physique of a competitive cyclist demonstrates that this form of exercise rewards the whole body. All muscles are taut and sinewy as they are in any other well-developed athlete. It would be impossible, in fact, to distinguish a bike racer from, say, an Olympic gymnast were it not for the biker's quadriceps, which are generally the size of a matched pair of steamer trunks.

Pick the cyclist.

Weight Loss

A person can control body weight through any of the various aerobic exercise programs offered by upscale fat emporiums. These are the places whose advertisements feature a woman with a body designed by a committee of thick-tongued adolescent boys. In bicycling, the method of weight reduction is unique. In a word, it is *friction*. The mechanics of a bicycle are such that with each revolution of the pedals a thin layer of fatty tissue is rubbed off from the inner thighs and buttocks of the cyclist.

You probably suspected that bicycle seats are not constructed strictly for comfort. You were right. These high-tech saddles are engineered primarily to enhance weight loss.

NOTE: As in any weight-reduction program, it is advisable to begin slowly and monitor your body's response. Certain signals will tell you that you are trying to do too much, too fast. In cycling for weight loss, it is a sure sign of excess when you notice that you've set your crotch on fire.

Spontaneous combustion caused by an overly ambitious weight-loss program.

Other Health Aspects

WARNING. The Center for Disease Control in Atlanta has spared no expense in determining that ownership of a bicycle has been linked to saddle sores, numb hands, backache, stiff neck, knee strain, leg cramps, chain rash, yellow fever, dog bites, insect bites, swollen glands, consumption, the plague, tonsillitis, acne, Rocky Mountain spotted fever, manic-depression, morning sickness, scar tissue, old age, East German measles, West German measles, seasickness, leprosy, unsightly facial hair, gunshot wounds, butterflies, labor pains, gum disease, nightmares, diaper rash, cigarette burns, and, finally . . . um . . . wait, it will come to me in a minute . . . oh, yes! Memory loss.

Chapter 2

History of the Bicycle

Creation

Physicists trace the origin of the bicycle back to the first split second of the universe. The Big Bang theory has it that all matter was created in one enormous explosion that would turn Muammar el-Quaddafi green with envy. The debris from this blast eventually coalesced into the galaxies, stars, and planets we know today. The implication, of course, is that all material things were present in essence at the very beginning. Atoms that would one day form tongue depressors and bazookas and control-top panty hose all burst into existence at the same time. Swarms of tiny bicycle molecules were hurled from the fireball, randomly spreading across space. Eons later they congregated and congealed to form the first American Flyer.

Evolution

Anthropologists offer a contradictory theory that the bicycle advanced slowly along with the evolution of man. The wheel, it is known, was developed by Osgood Oglethud, a Neanderthal by trade, around 211,914 B.C. Some months later the second wheel was created by a neighboring Cro-Magnon man. A lawsuit followed in which Mr. Oglethud, the plaintiff, claimed that Mr. Magnon, the defendant, was guilty of patent infringement. The dispute was settled out of court, since, at this point, courts had not yet been invented. Under the terms of the settlement, Mr. Oglethud became sole proprietor of the first two wheels in what could best be described as a sort of primordial corporate takeover.

With two wheels at his disposal it seems fairly certain that Osgood Oglethud must have bumbled onto the general principle of the bicycle if not specifically the Schwinn Varsity.

How Oglethud actually learned to ride, since he had used up his complete inventory and had nothing left to use as training wheels, is a question that puzzles anthropological historians. Historical anthropologists, on the other hand, couldn't care less.

Osgood Oglethud (left) road-tests the first bicycle.

Another point of dispute is whether Mr. Oglethud opted for side-pull or center-pull brakes.

Nothing much happened in history between the years 211,914 B.C. and the mid-nineteenth century A.D. Likewise, the bicycle remained unchanged until halfway through the eighteen hundreds. (See illustration for one type of machine popular during this era.) Stone wheels gave way to wooden wheels; handlebars and pedals became commonplace. But it was a single innovation in 1853 that launched the epoch of the modern bicycle.

Sir Reginald Penny-Farthing and his creation.

The Modern Bicycle

The simple addition of a playing card and a clothespin raised the bicycle from a mere curiosity to a serious mode of transportation. The card was attached to the bike with the clothespin in such a way that the card rubbed against the spokes when the bike was in motion. It made a noise something like this: **BLIBLIBLIBLIBLIBLIBLIB-LIBLIB.**

Suddenly everyone had to have a bicycle. Remember that this was the era of the Industrial Revolution and now the bike with its playing card sounded very much like the machines and motors that were coming into vogue. The bicycle became a favorite of high society. The lower classes enjoyed the machine as well, but they could rarely afford the playing-card option. They were forced to make the BLIB-LIBLIBLIBLIBLIBLIBLIB sound by pressing their lips together tightly and blowing. To this day, you'll notice, people who purse their lips, make motor sounds, and spray spittle are generally associated with the lower classes.

By the turn of the century the bicycle had essentially taken its present-day form. Wheels were composed of rims and spokes and pneumatic tires. The frame was metal, the saddle was leather, and the handlebar grips were rubber with colorful plastic streamers attached.

Social Impact of the Bicycle

The popularity of the machine forced many social changes. Dog owners were annoyed that public roads, which heretofore had been used for strolling peacefully with family and pet, were now jammed with panting cyclists in high-button shoes and knickers. In the summer of 1896 the Dog Breeders of America convened in Goosebreeze, Pennsylvania, to address the issue. The results of that meeting were noteworthy not just for their far-reaching success but more importantly for being the first documented case of genetic engineering. The breeders initiated an extensive program in which all canine species were trained to attack bicycles and devour them if possible. Docile breeds and meek throwbacks were eliminated, thereby making the hatred of two-wheelers a genetic trait. The campaign was so effective that today a dog that does not promptly attack a passing cyclist is either dead or, in reality, a cat.

In the early twentieth century the bicycle surpassed the horse as the most popular form of transportation. People were charmed by the fact that the bicycle did not require feeding, grooming, or special housing. Also, they didn't have to sweep up after it. Soon the horse was obsolete except for purposes of parimutuel betting and as the main ingredient in certain doggie treats.

These were the golden days of the bicycle. Bike makers tried to cash in on the popularity of the machine by offering all sorts of new variations on the basic theme. Orville and Wilbur Wright, brothers from Dayton, Ohio, tried to foist off a model complete with motor and wings. Bicycle purists, rightfully, would have nothing to do with the brothers' contraption. And though they did attract a few oddball followers, Orville and Wilbur remain but a footnote to bicycle history.

World War I

Not only was the bicycle a popular form of recreation and transportation, but when hostilities erupted in Europe in 1914 it became a battlefield asset. World War I ushered in a new era of mechanized warfare with tanks and machine guns and airplanes (or Flying Bicycles, as the Wright brothers insisted on calling them). But, to the Kaiser's men, hunkered down in their stinking trenches, the most dreaded sight of all was the rapid approach of a platoon of doughboys astride their Swiss Army bikes.

Decline of the Bicycle

By the end of the war America had fallen in love with the automobile. Suddenly the bicycle became as much a curiosity as it had been just a half century before. Fewer and fewer bicycles were seen in the streets. By the 1930s there were no more than fourteen bicycles in existence in North America. Where all those millions of bicycles went is anybody's guess, although scholars tell us it was most likely Peking.

By the 1950s bicycle sightings were so rare that they were usually discounted as being nothing more than misinterpretations of a natural phenomenon known as swamp gas. The United States Air Force was called in to study reports of bicycles mysteriously appearing behind a neighbor's garage ridden by aliens who bore a strong resemblance to Orson Welles. For several years there was a national panic over these sightings with incredible tales of innocent citizens being abducted by hideous creatures on tandem bikes who performed unspeakable medical experiments on their victims and asked them embarrassing questions about personal hygiene.

Hollywood capitalized on the hysteria with a string of B-grade

The Swiss Army bike.

horror flicks. Memorable among them were *Kiss of the Presta Valve, The Bride of Eddie Merckx, The Thing from Campagnolo, The Chrome Dropouts, Godzilla Meets the 7-Eleven Racing Squad,* and *Revenge of the Downtube Shifters.*

Even Congress got in on the act. Senator Joe McCarthy chaired the now infamous House Un-American Bicycle Activities committee (HUBA HUBA, as it was known in the press). Politicians and other performers were called before Congress to testify if they were now or had ever been owners of English racers. Every actor who had to his credit at least one male lead role in a Hollywood production and yet admitted to having ridden a girl's bicycle in his youth was blacklisted from all but liquid-bleach commercials.

Resurrection of the Bicycle

America, at this time, was a sedentary nation. But there were a few pioneers in the area of fitness who helped turn the nation's head with regard to physical exertion.

Theodore Cleaver of the television series "Leave It to Beaver" was seen by millions of children weekly. He became a role model for America's youth. He taught them that aerobic activities such as skipping rocks and kicking cans was socially acceptable behavior. He was even seen riding a bike on occasion and punching Larry Mondello in the stomach.

In the 1960s, President Kennedy encouraged, by example, participation in sports. Among his favorites were touch football on the White House lawn, sailing off Cape Cod somewhere near Walter Cronkite, and invading Cuba.

A few years later, Dr. Kenneth Cooper, who invented the United States Air Force, implored America to breathe hard.

But the final event that changed things forever occurred in the early 1970s.

The Oil Crisis

Although it was generally accepted that the American people had become the most powerful on earth, able as they were to order pizza delivered directly to their door, they were also vulnerable. For

United States citizens it had become impossible to move more than two hundred yards without the aid of a four-thousand-pound, 256-horsepower petroleum-fueled machine equipped with AM-FM radio, eight-track cassette player, and a sticker on the rear bumper proclaiming for whom the driver would brake. OPEC, the Organization of Petroleum Exporting Countries, decided to withhold oil exports to the United States because they were steamed over the portrayal of Middle Eastern natives in the movie *Lawrence of Arabia*. This oil embargo, of course, caused the price of gasoline to rise, the national economy to collapse, and, inexplicably, the careers of Donny and Marie Osmond to skyrocket. Americans were rightfully peeved.

Americans were forced to reconsider the bicycle as an economic mode of transportation. It was not an easy transition, since all but seven people in the Western Hemisphere had forgotten how to balance on two wheels.

The Bicycle Today

A revolution occurred in which Europe became the model for the United States. Soon, young Americans who had spent Sunday afternoons trying to identify the sticky objects under their car seats before sucking them with an industrial-strength vacuum cleaner, kids who had destroyed their fingerprints by excessively buffing their Buicks, and adults who had marked the passage of time with a Snap-on tool calendar were now behaving in a Continental manner. They used foreign words like *croissant* and Cuisinart (French for "loss of fingers"). They drank wine with their meals. They all went on vacation in August. And, once again, the bicycle became a practical and fashionable form of conveyance as well as an instrument of fitness.

Very few people read the history section of a complete guide such as this one. They usually skim over it and rush on to the nitty-gritty chapters. Because bicycling is a very serious subject, you're not getting off that easy this time. Please take out a piece of paper and number one to ten.

HISTORY QUIZ

1. TRUE OR FALSE. The Big Bang theory deals with overinflating your sew-ups.

2. What is the origin of *croissant* and what does it mean in English?

3. Did the Wright brothers have the Wright stuff?

4. What's the difference between an anthropological historian and a historical anthropologist besides salary?

5. Are you married filing jointly, married filing singly, or double-jointed?

6. What sort of bike did Theodore Cleaver's older brother, Eldridge, ride?

7. Compare and contrast the popularity of bicycling in the 1890s with the right to free speech.

8. In what year and in what country and on what bike did the first kickstand appear?

9. Name five things.

10. Which is larger: A twenty-seven-inch ten-speed or a ten-inch twenty-seven-speed? Explain.

Chapter 3

Choosing the Right Bicycle

Let's assume that you've read far enough and, yes, you are willing to cash in a certificate of deposit and invest in a bicycle. Choosing the right bike is a complex affair and requires much more study and deliberation than in choosing, say, your spouse. There are dozens of types of bicycles and there are basically only two types of potential mates: dominant and recessive. And while personal grooming, financial status, and dental records should be considered in a marriage, you must select from a nearly infinite number of combinations of bicycle components possible, the one set that you can live with forever. This decision is not one to be taken lightly and it is recommended that you consult with your clergyman.

TYPES OF BIKES

The Clunker

This basic bicycle is available only at garage sales and in your better neighborhood landfills. It is characteristic in its cast-iron frame, balloon tires, and rusty metal fenders with sharp edges, which are a favorite breeding ground for the tetanus microbe. It is a great beginning bike and you can usually pick one up cheap by trading away a driftwood clock or a used toaster.

The Mountain Bike

This machine is a newcomer to the cycling scene. It is distinguished by its cast-iron frame, balloon tires, and, frequently, rusty metal fenders with sharp edges. You may ask, "So what's the difference between a mountain bike and a clunker?" The answer is: five hundred dollars. What accounts for the high price? Development costs. A crack team of slick ad executives labored for many months with bicycle manufacturers designing a campaign to make big, heavy, poky bikes appealing to a public interested in only the lightest and fastest models. "An impossible task!" you exclaim. Remember that these same advertising experts had 160 million otherwise intelligent Americans proclaiming in one breath that they would like a burger with everything on it and that they were not a person named Herb. That kind of power is not only frightening, it's expensive.

The BMX

BMX stands for Bicycle Moto Cross. It is a machine designed for kids who care a lot about dirt-track racing and freestyle riding but aren't too concerned about spelling. The BMX is a small, sturdy, single-speed bike with a banana seat and is usually piloted by a certified juvenile delinquent. Police records indicate that 97 percent of all arson suspects escape the scene of the crime on a bicycle of this type.

The Stationary Bike

Bicycles, by definition, are meant to move. The term "stationary bicycle," like "military intelligence," is a contradiction in terms. There is no such thing.

The Tandem Bicycle

While tandems are built to carry two or more people, occupancy by more than fourteen is both dangerous and unlawful, except in Utah, where such ordinances are traditionally ignored to accommodate extended families. Believe it or not, a tandem bike is easier and

Crossing the English Channel on a balloon-tire bike.

The BMX bike and a certified punk.

more efficient to operate than a single bike. Two riders working in unison provide more power to the drive train. The additional weight improves stability. And cooperation between the riders allows one partner to relieve the other when needed. Problems can arise when the partners are of different political parties, incompatible socioeconomic backgrounds, members of rival street gangs, two thirds of a ménage à trois, or when their jerseys clash.

The Mormon Tabernacle Tandem.

The most serious trouble occurs when the riders are in disagreement over their route.

Tandems have the additional attractive feature that you can establish on them smoking and nonsmoking sections.

The Unicycle

The unicycle first appeared when a pair of tandem riders found themselves in serious disagreement over their route. Today the one-wheeled cycle is popular for its ease of maintenance. No gears, no

The origin of the unicycle.

brakes, no handlebars, no cables. And very easy to park. For obvious reasons, the unicycle is only 50 percent as difficult to master as a normal bike. The tough part is learning how to juggle and smile at gawking buffoons at the same time.

The Tricycle

A tricycle is an excellent choice for those who long to return to those innocent days of their youth. The trike is a very stable machine which provides a reassuring sense of security for its rider.

For those who are seriously contemplating the purchase of a tricycle, there are a few rules which are inviolate: Always stay on the sidewalk. Share with your sister. Never ride out of sight of Mom or Dad unless you have a note pinned to your chest which states that you are allowed to participate in cross-country tours.

The Spin Cycle

Closely related to the Rinse cycle.

The Folding Bike

For travelers with limited cargo space, the folding bicycle is an ideal option. Small wheels and strategically located hinges allow a full-sized, rideable bicycle to be stored in a backpack, an overhead compartment on an airliner, or in the bottom of a Styrofoam beer cooler. Rumor has it that the Japanese have produced a bike which collapses to the size of a silicon chip.

The Recumbent

This machine looks as if it emerged from the collision between a bicycle and a lawn chair. The rider pedals from a reclining position while seated in a chaise longue. There is an attachment for the optional Cinzano umbrella and a holder for a cool Long Island Iced Tea. Experts claim that this is the most efficient way to pedal a bicycle. Perhaps. It is undoubtedly a very efficient way to pedal blue-chip stocks.

The recumbent.

A footnote here. Recently a heavier-than-air flying machine attempted a solo crossing of the English channel. The aircraft was powered by a cyclist spinning happily in the recumbent position. The flight was a success although there was trouble when Soviet radar misinterpreted the craft as an incoming Cruise missile. World War III was averted only because the Soviet President was busy at the time, crushing Afghanistan.

The Touring Bike

The touring bicycle is the classic ten-speed, the Volvo station wagon of the cycling world. (See illustration, page 26.) If bikes were large enough to sport bumper stickers, most touring bikes, like Volvos, would editorialize with such opinions as: SAVE THE WHALES, STOP THE ARMS RACE, ARM THE WHALES, and so forth. Conservatives prefer mountain bikes attached to the top of a Lincoln Continental.

Many ten-speed touring bikes are actually twelve-speeds or fif-

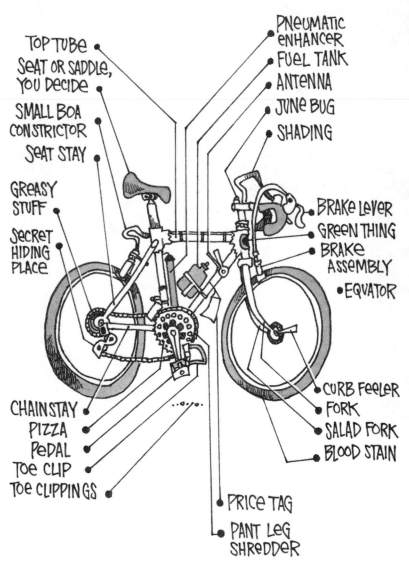

TOP TUBE

SEAT OR SADDLE, YOU DECIDE

SMALL BOA CONSTRICTOR

SEAT STAY

GREASY STUFF

SECRET HIDING PLACE

PNEUMATIC ENHANCER

FUEL TANK

ANTENNA

JUNE BUG

SHADING

BRAKE LEVER

GREEN THING

BRAKE ASSEMBLY

EQUATOR

CHAIN STAY

PIZZA

PEDAL

TOE CLIP

TOE CLIPPINGS

CURB FEELER

FORK

SALAD FORK

BLOOD STAIN

PRICE TAG

PANT LEG SHREDDER

The touring bike.

teen-speeds but never three-speeds although, in some circles, they may be five-speeds. The number of speeds all depends on the number of chain rings on the crank and the number of cogs on the freewheel. For example, if you have two chain rings and six cogs on your freewheel cluster then you have a total of two times six, or twelve possible gear selections. It should be noted here that it is possible to have a duplication of gears if you are not careful in selecting the freewheel arrangement. Suppose you have a thirty-tooth and a twenty-tooth front chain ring and fifteen-tooth and ten-tooth cogs on the freewheel. Riding in the "thirty–fifteen" is equivalent to riding in the "twenty–ten." Do you see why? Because experienced cyclists who wear shiny jerseys emblazoned with advertising logos would laugh at you, that's why. Also, nobody makes chainwheels with twenty or thirty teeth. Pretty complicated, huh? Be patient. This concept will be fully explained in a sequel to this book.

The Racing Bike

A racing bike is essentially a high-performance touring bike. The wheelbase is shorter, the angles in the frame a bit more abrupt, and the complete bicycle weighs just less than a dust ball. Track-racing bicycles have one fixed gear while road-racing bikes usually have ten or more gears. Before considering the purchase of one of these exotic machines you should be able to answer in the affirmative these questions:

A. Can I balance on two wheels?
B. Do I have $2,500 in pocket change?
C. Am I built like a Kentucky Derby winner?
D. Does a Republican occupy the White House?

You must now decide precisely which type of bicycle best suits your needs. Use the handy chart on the next page:

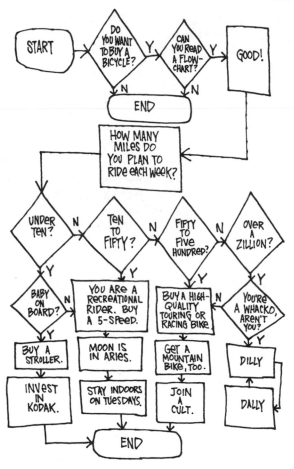

Flow chart to determine which type of bike you need.

After you have selected the type of bike you need, you must choose components for it. At this point you are going to encounter a lot of cycling jargon. Spend some time learning the official bicycle language known as Gearhead. The following list of words and phrases is just a sampling and by no means complete. For a more comprehensive introduction to Gearhead call or write the Berlitz School of Technobabble.

GEARHEAD

BONK: To bonk is to run out of fuel. It is easy to spot a cyclist who has bonked. He is usually crawling around on the highway looking for random complex-carbohydrate molecules or used bubble gum.

BREAKING AWAY: The title of a popular movie about stone quarries. It is also a popular bicycle maneuver.

CAMPY: Campy is short for Campagnola. Serious cyclists suspect that this is God's last name.

CHAMOIS: A small, deerlike animal native to the upper elevations of Europe and Asia. It is noted for its soft hide, which is used to line bicycle shorts. Hunting and trapping of the animals is unnecessary, since adult chamois commit mass suicide when they realize for what, precisely, they will be used.

COMA DRIVE: A mental gear that cyclists shift into when they are so tired they would rather be having their tax returns audited than pedaling their bicycles.

DROPOUT: A notched metal plate that has been welded to the frame for the purpose of securing the hubs and wheels to the bicycle. A dropout is also a cyclist who has decided that he can make more money in the Tour de France than he can by studying trigonometry.

DUST: To dust is to accelerate past a fellow cyclist with such authority that the other rider is forced to contemplate self-immolation or a career in the U.S. Post Office.

ENERGY PODS: Those puffy folds of skin at the waistline of inactive cyclists. Energy pods are where nutrients such as gorp are stored during the off-season. See GORP.

GORP: An acronym for "good ole raisins and peanuts." It is the chief form of nutrition for small woodland creatures and bicyclists.

GORP-HELPER: Any solid substance which, when added to gorp, makes it palatable.

HAMMER: To hammer is to ride at a speed sufficient to cause dogs and small children to seek shelter.

The chamois, upon learning its hide will be used to line bike shorts.

HONK: Honking is similar to hammering except that, unlike hammering, honking is restricted to downhill sections. On rolling terrain a strong rider is likely to hammer, honk, hammer, honk, hammer, honk, and so on.

PRIME: (pronounced *preem)* A special award given to the rider who leads at a certain landmark in a road race or at the end of a specific lap in a criterium.

PREEM: (pronounced *prime)* A special award given to a rider who best fills out a pair of bike shorts.

RAAM: RAAM stands for Race Across America, a grueling competition in which a score of riders pedal without sleep from southern California to Atlantic City, New Jersey, for no apparent reason.

REELING IN: To reel another rider in is to catch up to that rider because he is exhausted, you are riding stronger, or you know a shortcut.

ROLLING RESISTANCE: Anything that impedes the natural movement of a bicycle. For example there is more rolling resistance in a 1¼-inch clincher tire than there is in a 1-inch sew-up. And there is significantly more rolling resistance in a brick wall than in either of the above.

ROTH: ROTH stands for Race over the Himalayas. This competition is open only to survivors of RAAM who have also demonstrated a major decrease in the higher mental functions.

SADDLECTOMY: A medical procedure performed on riders who have committed themselves to a tour a bit longer than their bodies were willing to tolerate.

SLICKS: A bicycle racer's legs that are regularly shaved and waxed.

SUCKING WHEEL: To suck or catch a wheel is to align one's bike several inches behind another rider so that the wind is broken and the front rider does all the work. Ideally, each rider should share the burden equally by exchanging positions. In point of fact, this maneuver is successful only in socialist states.

TRACTOR BEAM: A ray emitted by a strong cyclist that attracts weaker riders and pulls them along behind.

WANKER: A person who dresses like Bernard Hinault but manages to avoid working up a sweat on a bicycle.

Now let's discuss bicycle components.

COMPONENTS

Let's assume that you've decided to buy a ten-speed touring bicycle. You could simply stroll into a retail outlet that happens to sell bikes such as the many well-stocked K marts around our nation and, once there, purchase one of their ready-to-ride bicycles. However, buying a bike that was stamped, cookie-cutter fashion, from a slab of pig iron, then shrink-wrapped in plastic with a cardboard backing and hung on a rack next to lawn furnishings may not appeal to you. If that is the case, then you should visit a bike shop. You can buy a ready-to-ride, off-the-rack model here, too. But all the salespeople would snicker and point at you. To avoid this embarrassing situation, you should confidently demand certain features on your bike. These features are called the components and when you become proficient enough to pronounce them all correctly the salespeople will regard you with respect. Following are the components you must learn to discuss.

Kickstand

A sturdy kickstand should be attached to the bike with a substantial bolt and boilerplate assembly, since light welding weakens the frame. The kickstand should be massive enough to support the bicycle in a stiff breeze or against the accidental nudge of an ice cream truck. A reasonable kickstand should weigh about 114 pounds on a good bike. The salespeople will tell you that "good" bikes don't have kickstands. Nonsense. They are simply trying to increase their profit margin by selling you less bike for more cash. They call it the Ten-Speed Golden Rule: "The lighter it is, the more gold it costs."

Insist on a kickstand.

Wheels

Wheels are an extremely important part of the bicycle. Without them you'd scratch up the bottom of your frame even on very short rides.

Wheels consist of tires, rims, spokes, hubs, and some other stuff.

Generally, there are two types of tires available today: inflated and flat. Major bike consulting firms suggest you use inflated tires. Flat tires are just about useless and, frankly, most experts are at a loss as to why there are so many of them in existence in this day and age.

You may equip your bike with clinchers (wire-ons) or tubular tires (sew-ups). A clincher is lined with a wire bead which holds the tire to the rim when the separate inner tube is inflated. A sew-up incorporates the tube and tire in one unit and is attached to rim with glue or, in emergencies, Trident sugarless gum. Sew-ups are lighter and more expensive than clinchers (see the Ten-Speed Golden Rule above) and they are able to take more pressure than clinchers, which makes them especially suitable for Type A personalities.

There are also two types of valves used to inflate tires. They are called Presta and Schrader after two extremely famous historical people. The type of valve you have on your tire is determined by the type of fitting you have on your pump. For example, if your pump is equipped with a Presta attachment, then your tires inevitably have Schrader stems. If you sneak out and try to correct this by changing to a Schrader fitting on your pump . . . Presto! Your tires are Presta. Don't fight it. Just ride on the original, factory-installed air.

The tire and rim are attached to the hub by a complex lattice of spokes. The spoke head anchors one end of the spoke to the hub while the threaded tail end is secured to the rim with a nipple that can be tightened or loosened to keep the wheel round. Wind-tunnel experiments have shown that round is better than triangular or square.

"Spoke," coincidentally, is the past tense of "speak."

There are many kinds of spokes . . . steel spokes, chromed spokes, butted spokes, and so on. You'll probably want to stock up on at least twenty different varieties. Here's a little tip: Instead of buying a complete set of every imaginable spoke, just obtain two of each type. Tear up some newspaper and place it in the bottom of a cardboard box along with a dish of water. Throw in the spokes and cover the box. In three weeks you'll have more spokes than you'll know what to do with. They are prolific breeders.

Rims come in steel or alloy, box-construction or seamless, heat-treated or cold-drawn, regular or diet. To the untrained eye there is absolutely no difference. Before setting foot in the bike shop, train your eye. Your finer health clubs offer exercise classes to help you do this.

As a protective device, hubs are designed to ooze dollops of grease that bear a striking resemblance to the Blob from the movie of the same name. It is known that bicycle thieves are the type who take these movies as gospel. A thief will give wide berth to any bike which is seemingly guarded by a carnivorous lubricant.

On certain hubs there is a lever that facilitates the instant removal of a wheel from the frame. These so-called Quick Release hubs are perfect for practical jokes. You can easily loosen a friend's hub and watch the wheel fall off when he pulls up on the handlebars while pedaling hard. It's good, clean fun . . . particularly if your friend is leading in the Tour de France.

The Drive System

The combination of parts that make the bicycle go is called the drive system. You, the rider, are part of the system. The energy you derive by burning such fuels as a fully digested corn dog or burrito supreme is transmitted through your legs to the pedals. The pedals turn the crank which conveys power, via the chain, to the rear wheel. The whole arrangement depends on the laws of physics dealing with mechanics, electromagnetic radiation, and certain aspects of Sir Isaac Newton.

The crank is the round thing about the size of a small pizza and is located about two feet below your crotch when you're sitting on a bike. It comes in four varieties: Cottered, cotterless, one-piece, and pepperoni. Its chief purpose it to snag pant legs or leave grease tracks on your right calf.

The crank arms extend to the pedals where you place the balls of your feet. For maximum pedaling efficiency your feet should be secured to the pedals. The traditional method involves wearing cleated shoes which are inserted into a rattrap metal cage, then cinched down with leather straps. Sounds kind of kinky, doesn't it?

In a recent innovation, bicycle manufacturers have borrowed an idea from skiers. A receptacle on the bottom of the bike shoe snaps into a spring-loaded binding on the pedal in the same way a ski boot attaches to a ski. A sharp sideways twist releases the shoe. This arrangement is not as erotic as the previous one but it can be enhanced with net stockings.

The ultimate system for securing the rider's feet to the pedals also borrows from an unrelated sport. In this case it's the fur trade, as illustrated below.

The chain connects the crank and the chainwheel to the gears of the freewheel. A cable, a rope, or a drive shaft would work as well, but the chain incorporates a special safety feature. On long tours, when the rider is lulled by the monotony of the landscape and rhythmic routine of pedaling, there is a tendency to fall into a deep slumber. This situation can be dangerous except in certain parts of Kansas. When the rider shifts gears, however, the chain makes a rattling sound which can be heard as far away as the Crab Nebula. This sound keeps the rider (and everyone else with normal hearing) wide awake.

High-tech pedal system using fur-trade technology.

The Gear System

On the crank there are two or sometimes three chainwheels. The freewheel on the rear hub usually consists of a cluster of five or six gear cogs. Both the chainwheels and the rear sprockets have teeth on them. You have a choice as to the number of teeth and their distribution among the gears. Your main concern here is that you sound intelligent to the staff of the bike shop. Here's how.

Memorize a list of numbers such as these: 52–12, 42–16, 42–21, October 12, 1492, 54–40 or fight, 15 minutes after 8.

Add them together. Then confidently repeat the digits to the salesperson. If the total exceeds the number of spokes on the bike by at least 220, minus your age, you've made a superb selection of gears.

Caution: Once you've bought the bike, don't think that you can simply forget this gearing numerology. You may be pedaling along comfortably one day, when you are pulled over by an officer of the American Gearhead Association who will demand to know precisely what gear you are in. Failure to respond within three seconds can result in a sharp rap across the knuckles with his frame pump.

Shifting gears is accomplished through a gizmo called a derailleur. A derailleur is obviously a French invention and consequently cannot be trusted. To make matters worse, most derailleurs are made in Italy or Japan. Recall that both these countries were our enemies in World War II. If you insist on buying such foreign components you run the risk of being called before a congressional subcommittee hearing, having network television cameras thrust in your face, and getting wired to a laugh meter to measure your degree of patriotism.

The derailleur moves the chain from one gear on the freewheel to another. There is a similar gear shifting device which moves the chain back and forth between the two front sprocket wheels. Both derailleurs are attached by cables to two control levers. The levers are located on the middle of the downtube where they are supposedly in easy reach of the rider. The cyclist can reach them all right, but only when he has his nose pressed against the handlebars. It is much simpler to sit back and let the gears shift around for themselves. Which they tend to do.

On some bikes there are shifters attached to the ends of the handlebars where they are supposed to be operated by the cyclist's pinky fingers. To operate anything mechanical with the smallest digits is laughable because pinky fingers are incapable of any useful activity other than probing the depths of one's ear canals. Experts contend that these shifters are actually not connected to anything.

Brake System

Look closely at a ten-speed bicycle. You'll notice four rubber rectangles about the size of pencil erasers located on either side of the wheel rims. These are your brake pads. Your life depends on them in an emergency. Life-threatening emergencies occur once every 3.7 seconds for the average cyclist. You probably expected the brakes to be a bit more substantial, didn't you? The idea here is to cut down on the overall weight of the bicycle. The brake system—pads, cables, calipers, and levers included—weighs slightly less than a Kleenex. To compensate for the system's dubious safety it is best to wrap your body in about three hundred pounds of foam rubber.

There are three types of brakes available on the general market:

A. The type that requires the grip of an enraged lowland gorilla to effect any noticeable change in the velocity of the bike.
B. The type that constantly rub against the rim whether you want them to or not.
C. The type that is strictly decorative.

These three brakes, taken together, are worth about a bucket of yak spit.

The Saddle

A bicyclist develops a deep personal relationship with his (or her) saddle. There is always a special place in his heart for the first one he ever had. Looking back, a rider may think of it as a comical affair, but, at the time, the experience was quite often very tender.

In choosing a saddle be mindful that never in your life will you be as close to another inanimate object. In fact, once you've actually consummated the bond, it takes a court decree to have it nullified. So take care, be extremely selective.

CeNTER-PULL BRAKe   SIDe-PULL BRAKe   LAND MINe

Devices used to decrease bicycle velocity.

Most saddles are made of leather. They eventually mold to your anatomy but require protection from dampness. Plastic seats are maintenance-free but tend to be inflexible. The best of both worlds, durability and comfort, can be found in the bean-bag seat. These saddles are so cozy that at the end of a lengthy tour a group of cyclists often stretch out in their seats and circle their bikes to form a conversation pit.

It takes a while to break a saddle in. During that time you will perspire and exude other semi-organic substances. These accumulate under the saddle in that dank area that never sees sunlight. You don't want to stick your face in there, any more than in the dim, musty corner of your basement behind the water heater. The same sorts of creepy things populate both places.

Bike shops generally stock a narrow selection of wide saddles and a wide selection of narrow saddles.

Steering System

The handlebars, stem, headset, and fork constitute the bicycle's steering mechanism. If you insist on getting technical, then you should haggle with bike-shop staff over the width, drop, and reach of the handlebars and the rake of the fork (or is it the fork of the rake?). The headset and stem are meaningless accoutrements and are mentioned here for snob appeal.

Your key concern here is tape. Although the subject is treated in

The bean-bag saddle.

detail in the fourteen-volume Encyclopedia of Handlebar Tape, the major issues are:

1. Should the tape be longer than it is wide?
2. Should I consult a decorator about color?
3. Should I have tight little spirally wraps or loose perky curls?
4. Should I tie the ends in a bow?
5. Once and for all, which sounds better: records or tape?

Frame

The frame is the skeleton of the bicycle. All other parts are attached like organs to the frame. You should be well versed in the structure, angles, and nomenclature of the frame before choosing one. Or enlist the aid of an expert such as a chiropractor or an Italian.

Frames can be made of steel, aluminum, chrome-molybdenum, or Formica. As of this writing, you are best advised not to select a chrome-molybdenum model for two reasons. First, both metals are

mined in South Africa, a nation notorious for its oppression of mi-
norities. And so you're liable to be stoned to death by college stu-
dents when riding near a campus. Second, the word "molybdenum"
is impossible to pronounce in the English-speaking world. Go ahead.
Try to say it five times, fast.

There are some terms you should know when selecting a frame.
Double-butted is one of them. Double-butted means the tubes which
make up the frame are thicker near the ends where they are attached
to other tubes. This kind of configuration makes the joints much
stronger and more resistant to punishment from riders who happen
to be double-butted.

On finer bikes you'll notice lacy sleeves of metal at each of the
joints. These are called lugs and they further strengthen the frame
structure even if they do make the bike look like the wrought-iron
fence that surrounds a bordello.

LUGGED FRAME

FRAMED LUG

Braze-ons are little fittings that allow you to carry bike accessories on the frame. Make certain your bike has attachments for a water bottle, tire pump, chainstay stop, down-tube bar end levers, bottom bracket left- and right-hand guides, top-tube cable guides, carrier mounts, drag chute, retrorockets, and cigarette lighter.

There are men's frames and women's frames. A woman may purchase a man's frame. But if a man wishes to buy a woman's frame, he must fill out a form which is kept on permanent file with the local vice squad.

Fitting the Bike

Once you've decided on a frame model and its components, you must select the proper size bicycle. Even off-the-rack bikes offer plenty of variation in dimension so that you may be assured of a proper fit (unless you are frequently mistaken for a Norge refrigerator).

The terminology used in fitting a bike takes getting used to. At one time the "inch" was the standard of measurement for most parts of the bicycle. But manufacturers suddenly realized that "inch" is an English word which is almost universally understood. And if everyone understood the language and concepts behind fitting a bike then the Professional Bike Fitters Union would be in an uproar. To correct this mistake the manufacturers made an exhausting study of the dead languages of the Tigris-Euphrates valley and came up with several alternate modes of calibration.

Frames are now measured in "cubits," wheels in "decibels," and cleated shoes in "angstrom units." Furthermore, instead of structuring this numeric scheme on the familiar decimal system (base 10), manufacturers and the Professional Bike Fitters Union have elected to base theirs on the uppercase "W." (For proper fit you should know your bodily measurements as described in the following illustration.)

Women will find that men's frames don't quite fit right. Even the so-called "lady's bike," without the standard top tube, is not proportioned correctly for female anatomy. Men and women are different. Generally, a woman has shorter arms and torso and longer legs than a man of equal height and she's not reluctant to let her emotions be

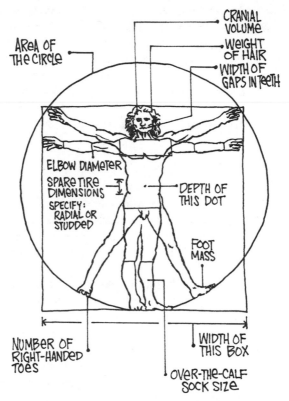

CRANIAL VOLUME

WEIGHT OF HAIR

WIDTH OF GAPS IN TEETH

AREA OF THE CIRCLE

ELBOW DIAMETER

SPARE TIRE DIMENSIONS

SPECIFY: RADIAL OR STUDDED

DEPTH OF THIS DOT

FOOT MASS

NUMBER OF RIGHT-HANDED TOES

WIDTH OF THIS BOX

OVER-THE-CALF SOCK SIZE

Key body measurements used in fitting a bike.

known during the tender parts of movies such as *Bambi*. Men prefer films like *Friday the Thirteenth, Part XII* because there is virtually no chance they will be caught blubbering in their popcorn when the theater lights come on.

Both male and female riders should follow the same frame-fitting procedure described below. A woman should buy the bike that best approximates a proper fit, take it home, then batter it with a two-by-four until it fits exactly.

NOTE: Some enlightened bike builders are producing frames designed specifically for women. But unless you are privy to the maker's past position on the Equal Rights Amendment, don't trust these products. Use the two-by-four technique.

If you are of average height, begin by straddling a 1.75-cubit frame bicycle of some desirable make and model. With your feet flat on the floor there should be about a half centimeter clearance between you and the salesman. If the frame is too small, you probably won't realize it and the salesman will sell it to you anyway. You will, however, know if the frame is too large by the fact that you cannot swing your leg over the top tube without an embarrassing injury.

A critical factor in fitting the bike is saddle height. An improper fit here can result in knee strain, back disorders, or, in extreme cases, acrophobia.

Measure the distance from the pedal spindle (when the crank is in line with the seat tube) to the top of the saddle. Now adjust until this length is precisely 109 percent of your inseam measurement when you are wearing toreador pants and heels.

The saddle may be tilted up or down for comfort. But stay in the safe zone. For instance, the nose of the seat is too high if you keep sliding off the back and getting your rump burned on the rear wheel.

The handlebars are also adjustable. You may cock them to the side so that they face north-northeast when you are traveling due south. Except as an attention-getter, there is absolutely no reason to do this.

By moving the handlebar stem up or down you can control handlebar height (don't do this while you are riding). Also, with your choice of stems you can determine the distance between the handlebars and the saddle, a distance which should not exceed the length of your torso or the Pennsylvania Turnpike, whichever is greater.

For those who are ordering a custom bike a few words: There are many more dimensions and specifications over which you have control. You can decide on the lengths of the top tube, down tube, seat tube, the chainstay length, stem length, length of the seatpost, wheelbase, fork rake, bottom bracket clearance, and the prime lending rate. These are things you don't want to order over the phone. Do it in person. Get it in writing. And, if possible, use a stolen credit card. (See accompanying pictorial guide for constructing your custom bike.)

All of these specifications for your custom bike are based on your personal body statistics according to formulas devised by the insurance industry. If you feel embarrassed about revealing certain details

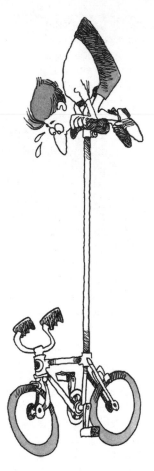

Improper saddle height may cause acrophobia.

of your anatomy to perfect strangers or you simply don't want to bother with all these picky details, buy a spandex stretch bike. One size fits all.

Building a custom bike: your step-by-step guide.

Color

Chances are you will own your bike far longer than the life of most prime-time television series. Popular detective shows may dictate fashionable colors for a time, but someday the stars of these series will be begging to do American Express commercials and you could be stuck with a teal-and-fuchsia bicycle frame.

Stay with the traditional hues. Pick up a color chart from your local hardware store or discount carpet outlet. Notice that eggshell white, avocado, and harvest gold never go out of style. Half the appliances in mobile homes across America are avocado. You can't argue with conventional wisdom like that.

Basic black is the most traditional color of all. With a yellow plastic water bottle and matching handlebar tape, your machine takes on a casual air appropriate for the streets or the bike rack. For formal occasions, a sequined tape job and a bottle of bubbly in the water-bottle cage transforms your bike into an elegant vehicle you'd be proud to park next to any Ferrari or Silver Cloud.

One last comment concerning components: You are probably bewildered by the variety of options and the myriad brand names from which you must choose. Just remember that you don't have to know everything under the sun about bicycles to make the right decision. You only need to know enough to guarantee that your bike is of slightly higher quality than the bikes owned by your immediate circle of friends.

Popular Models

By now you should have a clear notion of what you want in a bicycle. If you are still fuzzy about it, please review the previous pages and pay particular attention to those passages you highlighted with yellow marker.

We will categorize some of the most popular models of bicycle by cost. You need only find the price range that fits your budget to get an idea of what's available on today's market.

UNDER $500

Hahahahahahahahahahahahahahahahahahahahahahahaha . . .
you've gotta be kidding.

$500–$144,000

This is the range in which most of you will find yourselves. Coincidently, it is also the price range in which most bicycles are found. Another one of those little miracles of capitalism.

The comments concerning the bicycles listed below are the result of thorough road testing or vicious rumors.

THE GLOMAR GLOWWORM

This dandy little ten-speed is ideal for commuting or light touring. Equipped with quick-release handlebar bag, center-pull water bottle, and Reynolds 531 aluminum saddle, this bike represents an exceptional buy at just under $2,700.

SPECIFICATIONS:
Wow and flutter: plus or minus 15 percent (DIN)
Frequency response: 20–17,000 Hz
Optional Dolby Noise Reduction

THE ZITMOID XKG 7000

The 7000 is a mountain bike that replaces the classic 6999 model. But don't despair. This latest version is identical to the earlier Zitmoid with one added feature: In the hands of a seven-year-old child, the Zitmoid 7000 can be folded, twisted, and transformed into Godjello, the Death-Ray Robot from the planet Gruppo.

THE NISHIKAWA KAMIKAZE

The most popular Japanese-made Italian racing bike available to the general public. And with good reason. The care, craftsmanship, and expense invested in this bicycle's magazine ads are unprecedented in Madison Avenue history. The bike itself is no great shakes.

SPECIFICATIONS:
Weight: 42 kilos
Wheelbase: Varies with the terrain.
Tires: Two, if you're lucky.

Chainstays: Chain stays on about 40 percent of the time.
Suggested retail price: $7,699.95 assembled; $14.00 unassembled.

OVER $144,000

Now we're talking *good* bikes. We're talking about machines
whose tires are inflated with Campagnola air. Although these bicycles could very well be used for commuting they are better suited
for dangling from Elizabeth Taylor's charm bracelet.

There are pretenders to the throne, but in this category there is
really only one model:

THE PRINCE CHARLES

For overall style and bearing there is none better than the Prince
Charles (the women's model is called, naturally, the Lady Di).
Whether it's parked at a coronation or circling slowly behind the
lines during Empire expansion you will not find this bicycle wanting.
And can this baby handle! During royal processions it corners like a
dream. It's perfectly stable in times of palace intrigue and can accelerate in case of a coup attempt.

Price: If you have to ask you can't afford it. (Includes dealer prep.)

You are now fully prepared to make a choice. Either you decide
on one of the above models or you choose one on your own. The
latter option is discouraged, since the makers of the bikes listed in
this section paid a huge fee to have their products mentioned in *The
Ten Speed Commandments.*

You are now in the bike shop, checkbook in hand, about to make
the purchase. Stop. It's time to haggle.

Begin by affecting an exasperated expression and saying to the
sales manager, "I saw the same bike in a shop in Erie, Pennsylvania,
for half the price!" The manager will say, "So move to Erie, Pennsylvania." Shrug your shoulders and say, "All right, I will!" Then
promptly stomp out of the store. Walk very slowly up the street so
that the manager will be able to catch up with you before you reach
your car. He will then apologize and sell you the bike of your choice
at a 60 percent discount.

A few of you, very few, will find that this tactic does not work.
Perhaps you haven't learned your lines or the timing is off in your

delivery. Your eyes are darting about and your lip is dappled with beads of perspiration. For whatever reason the sales manager sees right through your ruse. In these rare circumstances you still have one face-saving maneuver left: You can move to Erie, Pennsylvania.

ACCESSORIES

Funny Little Painter's Cap

Strictly speaking, the cap is not an accessory. It is an absolute necessity if you are to be considered a serious cyclist. No one is quite sure what would dictate the use of precisely the same headwear for riding a bike and painting a house. Just be grateful that the same connection does not exist between cycling and, say, being a witch doctor.

There are four acceptable ways to wear the cap: bill up, bill down, bill in the front, bill in the back. Wearing it in any other fashion defeats the purpose of the cap . . . which is unknown.

Helmet

The helmet, unlike the cap, is functional. Its purpose is to determine how much heat the human skull can tolerate before it turns into Silly Putty. That's what the little mirror is for. You can monitor how soft your head is getting.

The hardshell helmet is made up of a high-impact plastic covering and a Styrofoam lining to absorb impact. A foam headband adjusts for fit and is designed to store perspiration for later release into the cyclist's eyes.

The leather hairnet variety of helmet is often preferred by racers for its light weight and superior ventilation. It offers little protection, but it does allow easy identification of the riders in magazine pictures.

Not to wear a helmet is to risk serious head injury in a fall. There are documented cases in which a helmetless rider has fallen, struck his head, and been left, for the rest of his life, with the mind of a punk rock deejay.

Pop quiz: Which is the unacceptable way to wear a bike cap?

Gloves

A proper pair of cycling gloves is padded in the palm area to protect against numbness. In 1986, 95 percent of all serious bicycle injuries were the result of numb palms. Numb palms have reached such epidemic proportions in this country that one comedian who isn't having much luck on the nightclub circuit intends to conduct a nationwide telethon on behalf of its victims.

Biking gloves are fingerless and open at the back of the hand so that riders develop a distinctive oval-shaped tan between the knuckles and wrist. This mark is for purposes of identification. Bike shops will not sell certain sophisticated items such as valve stem caps to customers who do not exhibit the official oval tan line.

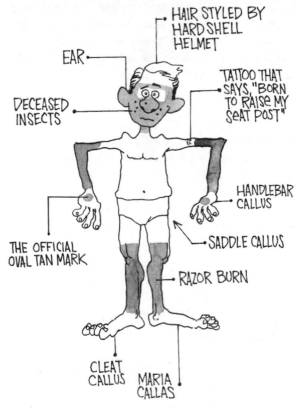

HAIR STYLED BY
HARD SHELL
HELMET

EAR

TATTOO THAT
SAYS, "BORN
TO RAISE MY
SEAT POST"

DECEASED
INSECTS

HANDLEBAR
CALLUS

THE OFFICIAL
OVAL TAN MARK

SADDLE CALLUS

RAZOR BURN

CLEAT
CALLUS   MARIA
CALLAS

The Cyclist's Tan and other distinctive bodily markings.

Gloves also come in handy when you run over some broken glass. You can reach down while you are riding and dust the tire with the palm of your hand. (For that matter you can do the same thing when you are *not* wearing gloves, since your palms are numb.)

Cycling Shoes

You can certainly ride a bicycle in an old pair of tennies, street shoes, or water skis, but your efficiency is enhanced by using specially designed biking shoes.

Touring shoes, although an improvement, are little more than stiff running shoes with reinforced soles. Maximum benefit comes from the use of cleated cycling shoes. These are commonly made of leather or nylon with a rigid shank in the sole and a plastic cleat on the bottom that makes you walk like a penguin.

Riding Shorts

Until just a few years ago the only place you would see skin-tight, shiny black shorts was in adult movies. Today they are part of the preferred mode of dress for even the casual cyclist. And no wonder. The elastic qualities of this clothing can, for instance, turn a woman who is constructed much like a Barnum and Bailey elephant act into the spitting image of Loni Anderson. Unfortunately it does the same thing for many men.

BEFORE   AFTER

The immediate slimming effect of riding shorts.

Not everyone should wear these shorts. There are some of us whose legs, encased in Lycra, look like a pair of sausages stuffed with Ping-Pong balls.

What is this miraculous material? Lycra is a member of the marsupial family and, according to one scholarly journal, it was brought to earth by meteorites. The world's supply of Lycra is concentrated in Milwaukee, and there is constant fear that a cartel will be formed to drive the price out of sight. Luckily, those who control the precious supply have been content, so far, to drink lemonade and listen to polka music.

A second important feature of cycling shorts is the padded area in the crotch. The padding is made from the supple hide of the chamois, a shy little fur-bearing creature that emerges from its den in the Alps once a year. If it sees its shadow, there will be six more weeks of the Tour de France.

Riding shorts are also available in wool. They were quite popular until the 1972 Olympics when competitors in the seventy-kilometer event were caught in a rain squall and the race had to be postponed so the riders could scratch for an hour.

Jersey

The bicycle jersey is a first cousin to the bowling shirt. They are both loaded with advertising and made from fibers not naturally found in this corner of the universe. These shirts are quite comfortable except when the temperature exceeds 65 degrees Fahrenheit. At that point a chemical bond is established between the jersey and the rider's underarms. Surgery is required to remove the shirt, although it is usually just an outpatient procedure.

Most jerseys are tailored with several pockets on the tail of the shirt, a convenient location for the cyclist. The rider's movement on the bike is not impaired even though the pockets may be filled with wallet, keys, water bottle, and such edibles as bananas, granola bars, and Irish stew.

Bicycle Pump

A floor pump with a pressure gauge is an essential piece of equipment. Before you venture out on the street your tires should be inflated in accordance with the following principle: The higher the pressure, the faster you ride. The faster you ride, the less time you have to make an intelligent decision in an emergency. Therefore, watch the gauge, and never inflate your tires above your IQ.

The frame pump is actually not a pump at all, since you'd have better luck inflating your tires with a baseball bat. The frame pump is, in reality, a combination back-scratcher and antidog weapon.

Lock and Chain

It is a sad state of affairs that a lock is a vital piece of bicycle equipment. Bicycle thieves are everywhere, particularly in Newark,

The best place to chain your bicycle.

where they have their own union, and Bike Theft is taught in the better trade schools.

A case-hardened chain or cable along with a substantial lock is no guarantee of security. But a thief may be thwarted if you make his job annoying. You can do this by snaking the chain in and out of the wheels and frame and wrapping it snugly around a policeman's leg.

You may want to consider, instead, one of the high-tech security systems. These are usually horseshoe-shaped affairs with a tubular bar at the open end. You encircle the frame and a portion of the bike rack with the horseshoe section, then snap the bar shut. If a person who does not know the combination to the lock tampers with it, an earsplitting siren will sound for up to three solid years depending on the state of the batteries. In addition, the thug will be sprayed with a fine mist of honey from a vial within the lock. Several seconds later a battalion of army ants is released from the tubular section and the thief is devoured in about a day and a half.

If you buy one of these systems, *do not forget the combination.*

Electronic Gadgetry

Today's bicycle computers are about the size of a cherrystone clam and are capable of surveying and directing the entire United States Strategic Air Command. With the touch of a button the rider can monitor his speed, distance, cadence, heart rate, retirement portfolio, and the activities of his fiancée while he's away on a long tour.

What's more, these incredible little doodads are often powered by solar cells that never need recharging except in Seattle. There are even a few experimental models that run on tiny nuclear reactors. They will be on the market as soon as developers can correct a certain bug in the system that frays handlebar tape and leaves the cyclist sterile.

Bicycle-Car Carrier

City dwellers will probably want to invest in a carrier. You can avoid unpleasant urban cycling conditions by driving to the country first, then beginning a bike ride. New Yorkers, for example, who plan to go for a spin, mount their bikes on their car racks (assuming they still possess a car in the morning) and drive three or four hundred miles until they are safely out of pistol range.

The bike computer before miniaturization.

The optional bicycle-car carrier.

Chapter 4

Riding Technique

Riding a bicycle seems easy. After all, it is an activity trained bears and monkeys master by two years of age. But these animals are much smarter than they appear. In fact several monkeys and bears were called in as consultants for this section of the book.

The Pre-Ride Check

Before racing, commuting, touring, or going for a Sunday pleasure cruise you should complete a preliminary checklist. First on the list, of course, is the question: Do I still own a bicycle? This concern may seem trivial but recent Justice Department statistics indicate trafficking in stolen bicycles is second only to the illegal flow of cocaine into Coral Gables, Florida. In other words more than fourteen trillion bicycles will be stolen in the time it takes for you to read this sentence.

Next, check your tires. Are they properly inflated? Clinchers generally require 60 to 90 pounds of pressure while tubulars take 80 to 110 pounds per square inch. If you don't have a pressure gauge, measure the length of time it takes to drive a thumbtack into your tire with a bass clarinet. Thirty pounds of pressure is roughly equivalent to four octaves at sea level.

NOTE: The correct way to inflate your tires is with a bicycle pump.

Trying to blow them up by mouth can cause brain damage. And never use the air supply available at service stations. The air is under such pressure that if you hold the nozzle of the air hose in place for more than two tenths of a second your tire will detonate. Also the type of people who hang around service stations are not amused by men with shaved legs and Lycra shorts. They are likely to heave empty Orange Crush cans at you.

Inspect your spokes. Make sure that they are equally snug. To do this, you "ping" them with your fingernail. They should all ring with the same musical note, D flat above high C. If you get something like Dueling Banjos, retune them with your spoke wrench. This is also a good time to make sure that you, indeed, have all your spokes. Count them. There should be about fifty or a hundred.

Grasp your brake levers. There should not be much travel between the open position and the fully engaged position. If there is, then you may need to adjust the brake cables, replace the brake pads, or ride uphill only.

Finally, look over the chain, crankset, freewheel, and derailleur system. If there appears to be plenty of metal and grease and wire down there and you're getting tired of all this preride nonsense, then you're ready to roll.

Mounting

There are several ways to get on a bike. The Tom Mix method requires that you station yourself twenty feet behind the bicycle which is propped in an upright position. Burst into a run toward the rear wheel, plant your hands on the tire, then vault into the saddle. (This method works better on a horse, where the saddle is more forgiving.) If you have already attempted the Tom Mix mount you are probably ready to try the Crusader approach. Like the heavily armored knights of the Middle Ages, you are very gently lowered to the saddle by a block-and-tackle arrangement.

The Traditional Technique is to swing your right leg over the top tube, insert your foot in the toe clip, cinch it tightly, press forward on

The Tom Mix mount.

the pedal, gain momentum, flip the opposite toe clip over so that your left foot can be secured, and all the while maintain your balance. The Tom Mix method is easier.

Gear Selection

Think of yourself as an automobile. Your eyes are the headlights, your ears are the doors, your nerve fibers represent the electrical system, your blood is the oil that hasn't been changed since before your last tuneup and therefore is clogging your oil filter, the spleen. Your nose is the air cleaner, your eyelids are the windshield wipers, your mouth is the glove box, your skeleton is the frame, that pimple on your cheek represents a ding in the fender. Your hair is a convertible top, your underarm is an ashtray. Tired of this metaphor? The point is cars have several gears to handle changes in speed and terrain. And since your body doesn't have them, your bicycle should.

Let's get technical. Most bicycles have between 1 and 118 gears. These many gears can present a problem. Unlike a car, there is no gear-shift knob on a bike with a convenient gear pattern printed on it. You must memorize the correct combination of lever adjustments to find the gear you want. Let's suppose that you have successfully mounted your bike and you are ready to select a gear. The simplest procedure is to pick your favorite number between 1 and 118. This

NUMBER OF TEETH ON REAR SPROCKET

NUMBER OF TEETH ON CHAINWHEEL

GEAR-INCHES BASED ON A 700mm WHEEL

Gear chart, simplified for easy memorization.

procedure works quite well unless your favorite number is 118, in which case you will blow out your kneecaps trying to turn the crank. A more sophisticated approach is to compute the gear ratios for each possible front and rear sprocket combination. This figure is then multiplied by the diameter of your rear wheel to yield the equivalent "gear inches" for each specific lever setting. The results are then divided by the gross national product of Bolivia while the square root of Tupperware is combined with a pinch of oregano. For a more detailed analysis, a Ph.D. in mechanical engineering from MIT is required. Put a bookmark here and return when you've earned your degree.

Back already? Good. Pick a number between 1 and 118.

Cadence

Cadence is the rate at which you pedal. For optimum efficiency and smooth riding you should strive to maintain a regular cadence. This rate will vary from rider to rider: 60 to 85 revolutions per minute are common for a commuter or someone on a bike tour. Racing cyclists will spin at 100 to 120 rpm. Scientists have recorded that one subject on a strict diet of Marlboros, Milk Duds, and Mountain Dew consistently achieved a cadence of over 575 for up to fourteen miles or to the nearest convenience store, whichever came first.

There is one very important rule to observe concerning cadence: If one foot is spinning at a certain cadence, say 75 rpm, then you must insure that the other foot is also spinning at 75 rpm. Violations of this statute are punishable by law and may result in a sentence of up to six months in prison and a severe limp.

Cadence and gear selection are closely related. If you cannot maintain your natural cadence in your present gear, shift to a gear in which this is possible. If you cannot do this you are worthless dumpster sludge.

Ankling

This is the method by which you entice fish to swallow pieces of wood which have barbed hooks attached to them and have been fashioned to resemble fish food.

No. Wait. That's *angling*.

Shifting Position

At some point you've probably wondered why the handlebars on today's bikes curve downward. Remember when you were a kid and *all* bicycles, including those flashy English racers, came equipped with handlebars that curved upward toward you, the rider? Those bikes were built for comfort. The handlebars were placed within easy reach just like the steering wheel on a car. (If cars were designed like modern bicycles, you'd be steering your Subaru from somewhere around your ankles.) Dropped handlebars (the contemporary kind) were developed following the results of physiological tests on laboratory rats.

Here is how the tests were conducted: Rats in professional careers with above-average incomes and vacation homes in the mountains were chosen because they had expressed a concern that they were neglecting the physical aspects of life in favor of the monetary side.

The rats were divided into several groups. One group took up racquetball, another started jogging, one bunch bought bicycles, and the control group remained sedentary, pouring all its energy into managing portfolios.

Researchers concluded that physical condition could not improve without a great deal of agony, and that rats do much better in the stock market than was previously supposed. So, in these health-conscious eighties the consumer of physical fitness equipment, including bicycles, is looking for something that will cause him tremendous suffering. Dropped handlebars do the trick.

It is essential, then, that you shift your grip on the handlebars anytime you begin to feel comfortable.

POOR   GOOD   EXCELLENT

Handlebar grip positions.

Breathing

Breathing is one of those touchy subjects, because everybody thinks he or she knows how to breathe properly. Okay, then . . . if *everybody* is such an expert on breathing, answer one simple question: Why are there so many dead people in the world today? Huh?

The basic breathing technique can be summed up as follows: in-out, in-out, in-out. Repeat as necessary. Memorize this pattern. There are many embellishments to this basic scheme. Look around you. Some people breathe through their noses silently while others make annoying whistling sounds. Then there are the mouth-breathers. These folks are usually slack-jawed, thick-tongued individuals who congregate around pornographic movie theaters. It is the latter method that is used in cycling.

Practice resting your tongue on your lower lip, dropping your jaw, and letting your eyelids fall to half-mast. See how relaxing that is! Add to this deep, rapid breathing and you've just about mastered it. The professional breather will add little personal touches such as creative ways to eliminate phlegm.

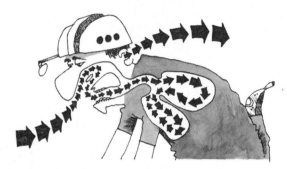

An advanced breathing technique.

Cornering

More bicycle accidents occur during a turn than at any other time. For this reason we suggest that for the first two or three years you ride in a straight line only.

When you feel experienced enough to make a turn, keep in mind several points. First, if you need to slow down, do it before entering the turn. Second, if the turn is too sharp for you to continuously pedal through, then keep your inside pedal high so that it does not contact the road. Third, it takes only minor shifts in body weight and handlebar alignment to complete a turn. Fourth, right turns and left turns are essentially the same except in Eastern Bloc countries and certain counties around Boston.

Climbing

Riding uphill is hard.

Riding uphill: how it feels.

Descending

Riding downhill is easy.

Riding downhill: a time for religious conversion.

Stopping

Learning to use the brakes is probably the most important lesson you will ever learn in your life next to long division. Besides routine stops, you will frequently find yourself in emergency situations in which you must rely on instinct to avoid disaster. You never know when a child or a car or a dog or a bunch of Shriners will suddenly appear in front of you. Some general guidelines will help you cope with these eventualities. Keep your hands near the brake levers at all times. Keep your center of gravity as low as possible. Keep, in your mind's eye, a picture of twisted metal, raw flesh, and shattered bone.

Dismounting

Once you've come to a full stop (unless you've impaled a Shriner) the dismounting procedure is as follows: Loosen the strap on your helmet, throw it off and say, "Whew!" Review your ride, taking pleasure in the wonderful ways the mind and body interact at the height of physical exertion. Blow your nose. It is important that these things are all done within three milliseconds of the time you stop because, as you recall, your feet are presently locked to the pedals.

The Post-Ride Check

Look yourself over. Are you all in one piece? Great. Throw your bike in the garage.

Chapter 5

Bicycle Safety

Illumination

Nine times out of ten if a driver spots a cyclist far enough in advance an accident can be avoided. (One time out of ten the driver will be at the wheel of a pickup truck and will deliberately inhale the cyclist through the radiator.) You can make yourself and your bicycle more visible with lights and reflectors.

Reflective tape is inexpensive. Buy a large roll. Use it on your helmet, bike bag, saddle, gloves, and shoes.

You can have great fun with the tape that is left over, too. Pick up a six-pack of wine coolers, a pint of strawberries, a strobe light, and a video recorder. Rent a motel room, get a date, and apply the tape liberally. Then use your imagination.

Reflectors help at night but nothing works as well as direct illumination. A small friction generator which runs off the spinning bicycle wheel can power a head- and taillight. Battery-powered lights can be attached to the bike frame or to the rider's arm or leg. Or, best yet, buy a neon-tube bicycle that flashes on and off with star bursts and arrows and a NO VACANCY sign.

Flags

Flags serve the same purpose as lights. They make you visible from a greater distance, sometimes for many miles, depending on the size of the flagpole.

There are some simple rules for flag use: If you choose to display the Stars and Stripes, you must carry a bugle. Reveille is at dawn, taps at dusk, followed by the traditional flag-folding ceremony. The flag should never touch the ground nor should it be flown below the flag of any other sovereign nation, particularly Disneyland.

Never fly the Israeli flag on a tour of Damascus.

Portable Radios

You have probably seen plenty of cyclists with portable cassette decks or radios stuffed in a jersey pocket and a set of earphones appearing from beneath a 7-Eleven bike cap. These riders are oblivious to traffic. Their heads are bobbing up and down and their bikes are swaying to the rhythms of Mr. Mister, Madonna, or some other purple-haired pre-adolescent with a diamond stud through its nose. *This is a very dangerous practice.*

Never, under any circumstances, impale your nostril with a diamond stud.

As for radios and cassette decks, the bigger they are the better. Just as with flags and lights, the sooner a driver sees a portable radio, the sooner he can take evasive action.

Storm Sewer Grates

Storm sewers have openings next to the curb and are covered with grates that run parallel to the flow of traffic. The slots next to the bars of the grate are exactly the right size to swallow a bicycle tire. When approaching a storm-sewer grate, you must align the bike with one of the bars rather than one of the slots. You can then safely ride over the grate.

An alternative method, for those who are a bit squeamish about the above technique, is to stop before you reach the grate. Get off

Use lights or flags to enhance your visibility.

and completely dismantle your bike. In as few trips as possible carry the parts of the bicycle to the other side of the grate by stepping over it. Reassemble the bike, then continue on.

Railroad Tracks

Riding over railroad tracks can be hazardous, particularly when crossing a set of rails that are also occupied by a southbound Super Chief. Now is a good time to employ the Jump Maneuver. Position your pedals horizontally as you near the tracks. Crouch low, then, when you are a few inches away, spring up while pulling on the handlebars and pedals. If properly executed, your leap should carry you and your bicycle safely to the other side.

If there's a flaw in your technique, you probably won't get a chance to remove yourself from inside the boxcar until you reach Mobile, Alabama.

Traffic

If you can, it is best not to ride in traffic. Avoiding automobile congestion, unfortunately, is only possible in remote sections of Antarctica.

Ride with the flow of traffic. Do everything you can to ensure that drivers are aware of your presence. The use of flags, lights, and radios has already been discussed. Other attention-getters include banging on the sides of passing vehicles with your frame pump, yelling obscenities into open windows, and ramming the lighter-weight Japanese imports.

Riding on streets lined with parked cars requires caution. Children are taught from infancy to dash out into the street from between parked vehicles and weave themselves into your bicycle spokes. A car door can suddenly swing open, demolishing your bike and sending you sprawling into the asphalt. This action is almost always intentional on the part of the driver of the particular car which, a few minutes earlier, you were banging with your frame pump.

After dark, approaching drivers have a tendency to leave their

How to jump railroad tracks.

high beams on as if a bicyclist isn't blinded in the same way another motorist is. Signal your displeasure by blinking your eyes violently.

Road Conditions

Be wary of any road which bears the sign, YOUR TAX DOLLARS AT WORK. Think back to when you filed your 1040. You conveniently forgot a little bit of interest income here and a cash transaction there. Maybe you even inflated a business expense. Shame on you. Just like every other American, you took a few shortcuts and crawled through every handy loophole. And you are just a small fry. Imagine how much money the big guys managed to hold back.

The point is, any road that depends on tax dollars to be built and maintained is going to fall miserably short of funding and will soon be pocked with potholes and strewn with gravel. Loose gravel causes falls, and entire bicycle clubs have disappeared into the larger potholes.

Unfortunately, all roads are built with tax dollars. Except private driveways. Do all your serious riding on private driveways.

Weather

On a bicycle you are exposed to the elements. It is in your best interests, then, to be well-versed in meteorology or cosmetology, whichever one deals with the weather. You should learn to identify cloud types. On tour with friends you should be knowledgeable enough to look to the sky and say with authority, "Yes, that one definitely looks like a steamboat."

Try to avoid rain, snow, hurricanes, tornadoes, dust devils, waterspouts, cooling trends, warming trends, high-pressure areas, low-pressure areas, the jet stream, prevailing westerlies, ground clutter, microbursts, gusts, sleet, an early frost, cold fronts, warm fronts, the Alberta Clipper, upslope conditions, chinooks, downslope conditions, humidity, and breeziness.

Ride indoors. Preferably in a garage at the end of a private drive.

Animals

Man is not the only living, breathing creature on this planet. We share the globe with millions of other species. Some are cute and friendly with soft, wet eyes and others are shy and withdrawn. No matter. All nonhumans, including some pedestrians and most joggers, should be herded into glass and metal facilities designed to keep them out of the way of cyclists.

Animals are nothing but trouble. And pets are the worst. At least a cyclist is warned by a highway sign that he is entering a deer-crossing portion of the road. But you'll never see a sign in the suburbs that reads HAMSTERS AT LARGE. And so you're peddling along contentedly when, suddenly, *squish,* you've run over a hamster. You lose your balance, plow into the pavement, and you are instantly surrounded by a horde of bawling children who are pointing their fingers at you. Perhaps in revenge the parents release their larger pets, the ones with blood lust in their hearts. And now you are in the race of your life. You collect yourself and sprint out of town with gnashing teeth and tentacles and fangs snapping at your ankles. You escape but only through the miracle of adrenaline.

And then you have to deal with the ugly hamster stain on your front clincher.

Thermonuclear War

To be precise, thermonuclear war should be listed as a subcategory under Road Conditions. Certainly a nuclear exchange affects your riding surface. But there is much more. You must confront wind gusts up to 300 miles per hour and temperatures approaching 8,000 degrees Centigrade.

The rules are simple in a nuclear situation. Ride with the wind. Don't fight it. Drink plenty of fluids because of the heat; a minimum of two water bottles. Pedal away from the superpowers. Try to reach a neutral country.

The Missing Man Formation.

BICYCLE ETIQUETTE

1. Always ride on the right side of the road or bike path. Pass on the left. Laugh derisively when you pass.

2. Yield to those with a higher station in life, such as a religious figure or a monarch.

3. Warn other cyclists, pedestrians, and motorists of your approach by sounding a bell or horn or howling like a coyote.

4. Obey all traffic signals and signs if there is a policeman present.

5. Ride single file in a group. The only exception to this rule is when a member of your group has recently been snuffed out by a delivery truck. You may then ride in the Missing Man Formation.

6. Learn the four basic hand signals: "I'm turning right," "I'm turning left," "I'm slowing down or stopping," and "I'm a single white male, 38, seeking SWF, 25–35, who would like to share intimate evenings listening to motivational tapes and drinking milk."

7. Give the right of way to anything larger or more menacing than you.

8. Do not ride for thirty minutes after eating. Do not eat for thirty minutes after riding. Chew your food.

9. Report all bicycling accidents to the local authorities. Also report any suspicious-looking vehicles, gatherings of two or more members of a minority, or anything else that just doesn't seem right to you.

10. Don't double-date with large people on a single bicycle.

Chapter 6

Commuting

Riding a bicycle to work is a wonderful alternative to driving a car or taking the bus. Not only do you save gas money or bus fare but you benefit from regular exercise. You arrive at your workplace refreshed. And, at the end of the day, your trip home is a great tension-reliever. Bicycle commuting is highly recommended to all but the unemployed.

Equipment

The single most important piece of equipment for the bicycle commuter is the rubber band. Use it to secure your pant legs tightly around each ankle to prevent your clothing from getting caught between the chain and chainwheel. Make certain the rubber band is large enough not to cut off blood circulation to your feet, which you will need once you arrive at your destination.

Pacing

A leisurely routine is a serious part of commuting. Suppose you live ten miles from your place of employment. Allow enough time in the morning to shower, eat a light breakfast, slip into your Halston original or your Armani suit, strap your briefcase onto the luggage carrier, and still make it to work by nine o'clock without having to

The joy of bicycle commuting.

ride the equivalent of an Olympic-qualifying time trial. Set your alarm for 3 A.M.

Some commuters prefer to get in a vigorous workout during their morning ride. You know the type. They are the ones who can clear an elevator or a crowded office in the amount of time one usually reserves to describe events on the subatomic scale. These are the people who are personally responsible for the deterioration of the ozone layer. If you are one of these folks, have the common courtesy to find work in a steel mill.

On the Streets

More and more municipalities are building bike paths. (Check accompanying atlas for America's major bike paths.) These asphalt trails would make wonderful commuter thoroughfares if it were not for the fact that they tend to circle parks. How many of you work in a park?

There is no way to avoid it—you will be forced to ride on city streets, at least part of the way.

City-street riding can be thrilling. There is nothing quite like the rush you feel when you are passed by a diesel bus just a millimeter or so away from your elbow. Because buses make frequent stops you are

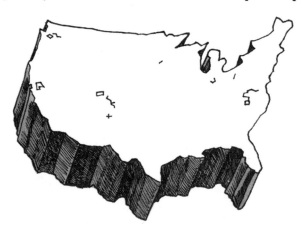

The major bike paths of America.

likely to leapfrog your way downtown with the old Number 15. You and the driver will get to play games with each other. He will sneak up behind you and try to clear your lower digestive track with his air horn. You will sign your name on the side of his bus with a tire tool. He will test your reflexes by forcing you into oncoming traffic. You will race ahead, hide your bike in the bushes, board the bus, and stab the driver to death with a spoke.

The bicycle commuter does not often win in these confrontations. In fact the average lifespan of such a commuter is identical to that of a forward artillery observer in a Southeast Asian war zone.

If you are one of the unlucky ones, the kind that has had so many collisions that you qualify for the Bicycle Commuters Frequent Flyer Program, then follow this advice: Next time, try to write the offender's license-plate number in blood on the pavement so that homicide detectives can begin their investigations with a solid clue.

Security

Let's assume you've made it downtown. Granted, that's a major assumption. You can either lock your machine to a bike rack or keep it in your office. If your career consists of selling Orange Julius from a beverage cart, the second option is out.

No matter how hefty your cable or how rugged the bike rack, thieves will find a way to succeed. Consequently, you must personally check on your bike every twenty to thirty seconds during working hours.

Chapter 7

Touring

There is no better way to see this or any other country than by bicycle. It is the ideal way to take a vacation.

If you travel by car you miss so much. Your eyes are glued to the highway or the rearview mirror. You are constantly trying to make "good time" by flagrantly violating the speed limit, depleting our precious oil reserves, and exposing the soft underbelly of this fine nation to the petroleum-exporting countries. This is nothing short of treason. You should be marched up against a wall and riddled with bullets.

Air travel is even worse. Your sightseeing consists of listening to static from the cockpit: "Passengers on the left side of the aircraft can see parts of Montana below. Or maybe that's Baltimore."

Airline food is legendary. A normal-sized sirloin steak is genetically altered and called "salmon." It is then divided 125 ways among the passengers and served with poisonous mushrooms and a croquet ball disguised as a roll.

Above all, you have to question any mode of travel in which a vomit bag is standard equipment.

Touring by bicycle allows you to see so much more and in such great detail; a raccoon, for example, that's been run over by a Greyhound bus. You share your sense of existence with the road kill. You are on intimate terms with the highway. You get in touch with gravel. You are at one with the no-passing zone. The white line becomes a part of you (usually, in a fall, part of your shoulder).

The economics of bicycle touring is also appealing. Once you've paid $1,500 for the bike, $725 for the special luggage required, $932 for lightweight touring wear and shoes, $2,671.95 for weatherproof sleeping bag, tent, and camping equipment, $175 in tools, and $692 for freeze-dried approximations of food, touring is FREE!

What You Need

1. First, you need a sound bike. Your regular ten-speed should do fine. If your tour involves climbing the World Trade Center you will have to include alpine gears on your freewheel cluster. One gear cog should be at least the size of a manhole cover.

2. *Clothing.* You should be prepared for all eventualities. Last year, one tour group on an overnight summer ride around Tucson, Arizona, woke up, unaccountably, in Finland. In their haste, they had failed to pack parkas! Search parties found them huddled together, frozen, with signs that wild starvation had driven them to eat the chamois out of their shorts.

Always pack these items: A cotton cap, a wool hat, and a propeller beanie. Sunglasses that block out harmful ultraviolet rays. Collarless shirts (collars tend to whip around in the wind and cause facial lacerations). Shorts. Swimwear. Evening wear. Smoking jacket. Trench coat. Tam o'Shanter and kilts. A sock. Another sock, which does not have to match the first sock, since this is not a fashion show. Needle, thread, and a loom.

3. *Emergency Kit.* Be prepared for mechanical failures both on your bike and on your body. For your bicycle you'll need a screwdriver, spoke wrench, tire irons, spare tubes, freewheel remover, chain rivet remover, fingernail polish remover, brake cables, rim tape, patch kit, spokes, radial arm saw, pocketknife, jumper cables, vegematic, Allen wrenches, and Allen.

Your first-aid kit can contain every liniment, ointment, and unguent known to medical science. You can stock every possible dressing, a stretcher, a blood pressure cuff, an iron lung, a CAT scanner, a dog scanner, a cure for cancer, rubber gloves and K-Y jelly, an anesthesiologist, a rude receptionist, and three-year-old copies of *Field and Stream* and *Reader's Digest.*

You can do that or you can take the modern approach: Double your medical insurance. Nervous insurance adjusters armed with Uzi submachine guns will surround you like a squad of Secret Service men and protect you from any harm.

4. *Food.* You only need two types on a bicycle tour. Gorp is one. Gorp is a substance that can be obtained in your local pet shop. Parakeets are particularly fond of it. It is not fit for human consumption and that is why you must carry the second item, Gorp Antidote.

5. *Miscellaneous.* Personal identification in the form of military records, birth certificate, or a distinguishing scar or tattoo. Money. Cooking gear, sleeping bag, and tent. No-pest strip. Water bottles. Maps, compass, and airline tickets home. And to record the whole memorable experience, don't forget to include a camera or sculpting tools and a block of granite.

You will also need something in which to carry all this gear. If you can fit it all in a fanny pack, great. It's more likely you'll need a seat pack, handlebar bag, and panniers. You may even find yourself employing the services of the Mayflower moving company.

If you can swing it, a sag wagon is a wonderful luxury. A sag wagon is a van or large, American-made sedan which carries most of the supplies. It relieves the riders of cumbersome loads and provides a place for an exhausted cyclist to recover. The sag wagon customarily follows the riders at a safe distance. For seven or eight hours at a stretch the van will creep along the highway at speeds approaching eleven miles per hour. It takes a unique type of person to drive a sag wagon. That special breed is highly amused by such activities as watching yogurt go bad or calling roll in Asia.

Ways to Travel

1. *Solo.* Like scuba diving, where the dangers are so grave that the buddy system is used, cyclists tour in groups of two or more. No cyclist wants to get caught by himself in the midst of a school of flesh-eating fish.

Occasionally you will see a single rider festooned with Gore-Tex

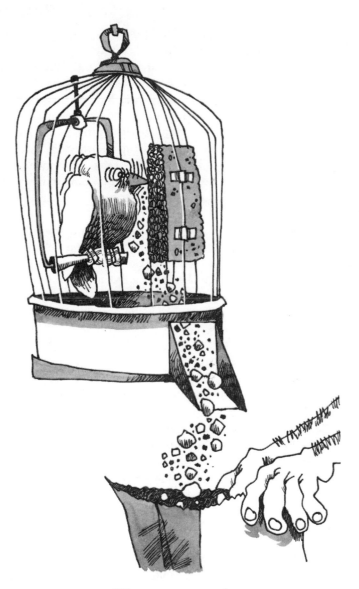

Where gorp comes from.

packs and pricey camping gear. That person is not on a bike tour. That person has just burglarized the local Eddie Bauer's.

2. *Organized Groups.* This is an ideal way to get started. Every major city has at least two or three clubs. Join one. The chess club, the Future Farmers of America, a quilting bee—it doesn't matter. The important thing is to infiltrate one of these organizations and systematically bend their will. Begin by dropping hints that their specific activity has been linked with skin disorders in laboratory animals. Follow through with rumors that Don Johnson has taken up bicycling. And so have Ed McMahon, Sean Penn, Willie Nelson, Frank Sinatra, Mario Cuomo, Nancy Reagan, Ally Sheedy, and Cher. But not Joan Rivers.

Before you know it, these people will have given up their jobs and families and their deepest personal convictions in order to devote themselves to cycling and to you. If you have a certain flair you might get them to invade Czechoslovakia. At a minimum they will conduct some first-class bike tours.

3. *Disorganized Groups.* These are made up entirely of bipartisan congressional subcommittees.

Popular Routes

A wonderful thing about bicycle touring is that there is a multitude of routes available to cyclists. Whether you follow a prescribed path or make one up as you go, the variety of possibilities is overwhelming. You may travel through forests, over mountains, across deserts, round and round red-light districts. Whatever excites you.

What follows is an atlas and guide to some of the finest bicycle tour routes on this planet. Each one has been ridden, mapped, and recorded by an expert recognized by the membership committee of the National Congress of Respectable People.

The material below is compiled merely for the purpose of making this book complete. No guarantees are implied as to road conditions, prices, or the accuracy of the information. The routes described here were pristine when they were examined. In order to keep them that way you should not tell anyone about them. In fact, don't even ride them yourself.

TOUR OF THE OKLAHOMA WINE COUNTRY

Distance: Endless

Bicycling time: About an eon and a half

Terrain: Imagine, if you will, a butcher-block table stretching from horizon to horizon.

Difficulty: Agonizing. It's like a bad dream in which you are riding through glue and an enormous creature in bib overalls is chasing you, getting closer and closer, and finally he drowns you in tobacco spittle. Those who have completed this ride have often required institutionalization.

Points of Interest: A tree was reported to exist about fourteen miles north of Norman, Oklahoma.

Allow yourself to be lured by the siren song of Oklahoma, the lyrics of which are present on every license plate in the state: "Oklahoma is Ok." A charming thought brought to you by the Oklahoma City Chamber of Commerce Advanced Think Tank.

This strenuous tour is a loop course and so any spot will make a

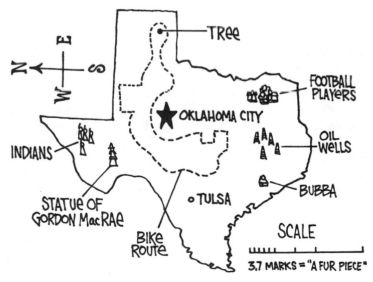

Detailed, up-to-date route map of Oklahoma.
(courtesy The American Gearhead Association)

Oklahoma's most popular landmark.

fine starting point—the Texaco station in Tawhuska, the stoplight in Uncas, Vern Waggoner's manure wagon in Putnam. It doesn't matter.

Pedal directly to the fairytale land of the Tulsa wine region. Take time to tour the renowned vineyards. Foremost among them are the cellars of Ernest and Julio Iglasias, Chateau Bartlesville, and Bubba Joe Poluski's House of Wine and Bait Shop.

Bubba never fails to invite passing cyclists in for a tasting of his noble Sparkling Comanche White. Be aware that there is a certain ceremony to these occasions. Bubba begins by leaning against an RC Cola machine, squinting into the sun, and taking a long, hard pull on a bottle of his finest. Before passing it to you, he wipes the mouth of the bottle with his sleeve. You should do the same. Mimic each of his gestures, which invariably include lazily clawing at his crotch and kicking the dog.

If Bubba takes a shine to you, he may conduct you on a grand tour of his wine-making process. Don't pass up this rare opportunity. It only takes about fifteen minutes. Watch him crush the grapes with a '54 DeSoto, strain the juice through a fishing net, and add the hair tonic.

You can repay Bubba for his hospitality by purchasing some bait.

Back on the road again, fortified by Bubba's nectar, be careful not to plow into a cow. Continue pedaling until you arrive at something interesting, which should take you into the next time zone.

THREE MILE ISLAND COASTAL TOUR

Distance: Three miles
Bicycling time: About the same as the half-life of Strontium 90
Terrain: Flat and well-illuminated (it glows)
Difficulty: Spinning along is hindered somewhat by having to wear lead-lined biking shorts.
Points of Interest: To this day hundreds of executives and government officials still mill around and point at each other.

Begin the tour at ground zero. Use the tall cooling towers to orient yourself. Head directly to the water's edge.

This place is a seafood lover's delight. Every imaginable form of marine life has washed up on the shore of Three Mile Island. All yours for the taking.

The Three Mile Island Coastal Tour.

Even on a cloudy day here, it is wise to cover your exposed skin with a number 15 sunblock. As beautiful as it is, with so many colorful isotopes and mutant forms of wildlife, don't linger. If you begin to feel some chromosome damage, call it a day.

The Three Mile Island Coastal Tour is a perfect training ride for the more extensive Ride-the-Ukraine sponsored by the Optimists of Chernobyl.

THE GRAND PRIX OF BEIRUT

Distance: Forty miles
Bicycling time: It varies. Two hours to eternity.
Terrain: Ever changing
Difficulty: Not too bad if you armor-plate your bicycle
Points of Interest: The rubble that was once the U.S. embassy, the rubble that was once American University, the rubble that was once the airport terminal, the rubble that was once the Holiday Inn.

Beirut is situated in the heart of the Middle East, which is conveniently located at the juncture of Europe, Africa, and Asia. Getting to Beirut is not as difficult a task as you might think. First, transport yourself and your bicycle to Europe, which is probably the best known nearby landmark. Make your way to the Mediterranean and hang out on the docks or in an airport. Casually let it be known that you are an American. Within minutes you will be on your way to Beirut as guests of one liberation front or another.

Once there, thank your hosts for their hospitality and explain that you are on a bike tour and must part company with them. Say this in pleasant, even tones as you back out the door. Don't make any sudden moves.

The first thing you'll notice is that the road conditions are less than standard. Equip yourself with puncture-resistant tubes and constantly dust your tires to rid them of annoying shards of shrapnel. A fun thing to do in Beirut is to stop frequently during the ride and try to identify members of various factions and splinter groups. A pair of binoculars and Audubon's *Field Guide to Terrorism* make this fairly safe sport.

A more daring approach is to actually pedal up next to one of these characters and say, "I see, sir, by your facial hair, that you are a Christian Phalangist!" and proudly point to the illustration in the Audubon guide. If you are correct, you and your whole group will dine sumptuously on stuffed grape leaves and couscous, swill great quantities of red wine, and swap stories around a campfire with heavily armed and slightly crazed-looking people.

If, instead, the gentleman is a Shiite Moslem, offer a thousand pardons and sprint out of mortar range.

Bicycle touring in Beirut.

Beirut offers the finest open-air eating establishments in the world. Alas, it is not by design. All of their establishments, photographic darkrooms included, are open-air.

Pull up to any one of these charming little bistros for your midday meal. Park your bike nearby and watch cute little street urchins frolic around it. Be vigilant, though. One of their favorite playful pranks is to replace your frame pump with a pipe bomb. Order a light repast and marvel at the fireworks for which this city is renowned.

Leaving Beirut is a bit more difficult than getting there. It could involve some high-level negotiations initiated by the Reverend Jesse Jackson. It could require the intercession of Amnesty International, the Red Cross, and the United Nations. Or it could be as simple as calling in the First Marine Division.

Without going into detail, here are a few more tours for your consideration: The Annual Great Bike Ride Across Rhode Island (TAGBRARI), the Street Tour of Venice, the South Bronx Obstacle Course, the Bataan Death March, the Ho Chi Minh Trail, the Northwest Passage, and the Yellow Brick Road.

Some Random Rules for Bike Tourists

Eat lightly before riding. If you gorge yourself on a large breakfast and then begin pedaling, the blood goes directly to your muscles. The food in your stomach decays and you eventually explode.

On long-distance tours always adjust your mileage for continental drift.

In countries in which you are not fluent in the native language, speak loudly. Everyone understands volume.

It is well known that there are no paved roads in the Third World.

If in trouble in a foreign country, seek diplomatic immunity.

If in trouble in the United States, claim executive privilege.

Riders who choose to tour the back country on mountain bikes, beware: Don't eat those things that look like raisins.

Take short frequent rests; avoid alcohol, meat, and tobacco; don't force the pace; drink often; brush after every meal; and remember Grandma in your prayers.

Chapter 8

Racing

If art, to you, is a poster of Davis Phinney, Greg LeMond, or Rebecca Twigg; if you leave chain links lying around next to the chips and dip; if you've ever accidently mistaken the sew-up glue for toothpaste, then you are what is called an avid cyclist.

As an avid cyclist you've probably considered the idea of bicycle competition. Racing is a natural extension of the efforts familiar to you as a commuter or tourist. But to take this step requires mental as well as physical stamina.

It also requires sacrifice. To race successfully you must train hard and give up the pleasures that mere mortals enjoy. You can't sleep in on Saturday morning. You can't take part in social affairs. And you lose your right to vote.

The following test will determine if you are truly made of the Racer's Stuff:

1. When I'm alone I enjoy:
   a. "Laverne and Shirley."
   b. catching up on back issues of the *New England Medical Journal.*
   c. getting in touch with the cosmos.
   d. pounding on my thighs with a meat tenderizer.
2. As a child I was most afraid of:
   a. the dark.

    b. my older sister.

    c. Richard Nixon.

    d. losing contact with the pack.

3. When I have a disagreement with a friend, I:

    a. take time to understand his point of view.

    b. sob uncontrollably.

    c. storm off in a snit.

    d. slice his clinchers.

4. My friends describe me as:

    a. warm, sensitive, sympathetic.

    b. cultivated and intelligent.

    c. attractive, funny, the life of the party.

    d. a good climber.

5. I'm secretly thrilled by:

    a. exotic dancers.

    b. black lingerie.

    c. nude swimming.

    d. guys with shaved legs.

6. When in a group, I like to:

    a. take charge, lead the discussion.

    b. listen and learn.

    c. tell amusing anecdotes.

    d. draft.

7. What I appreciate most in a member of the opposite sex is:

    a. nice looks.

    b. a pleasant personality.

    c. wit and charm.

    d. a good floor pump.

8. Nobody knows that I'm really:

    a. shy.

    b. insecure.

    c. reserved.

    d. training twice a day.

9. Complete the following phrase: Camp . . .

    a. David.

    b. Pendleton.

    c. Kitchykiwi.

    d. agnolo.

10. At the end of a long day I:

    a. kick off my shoes and watch the news.

    b. sip brandy and fire up a stogie.

    c. lose myself in a good murder mystery.

    d. sprint.

Did you pass the test? Good. Now it's time to quit your job and sell the children. Racing is a full-time endeavor.

TYPES OF RACES

In bicycle racing, as in tax accounting, to specialize is to excel. It follows that if your specific event is obscure enough you have a very good chance of being the best in the field. For example, if you decide to devote your life to circling hot tubs on a Big Wheel, you have a better than even chance of going down in history as the king of that particular sport.

What follows is a list of the more traditional forms of racing. Pick one that suits you.

Cyclocross

This is a rugged event in which the racer rides his bike through mud, across stagnant bodies of water, over logs and boulders, up staircases, and through storm sewers. Understandably, this branch of the sport is not very popular in the United States. Europeans love it. But then, they have different standards of cleanliness.

Bicycle Moto-Cross

In bicycle moto-cross kids dress up like motorcycle racers, ride bikes that look like motorcycles, and chase around on motorcyclelike race courses. They are required to affect the mannerisms of Marlon Brando in *The Wild One* and wear black outfits decorated with skulls and knives.

As if you couldn't have guessed, this sport originated in California.

Track Racing

Track racing is a very specialized branch of the sport. Races take place, for the most part, on banked oval tracks called velodromes, which are found mostly in underdeveloped countries and Shakopee, Minnesota.

Everything is done to make track bikes speedy. The bicycles are equipped with just one big gear and no brakes (not recommended for mountain tours). Instead of normal wheels, these machines are fitted with what appear to be 78 rpm recordings of Tommy Dorsey's greatest hits. These discs help the racer with his rhythm.

The rider is also dressed for speed. He wears a slippery body suit and, for a helmet, he straps on the nosecone of a Minuteman missile. Rather than using traditional bicycle cleats, the racer wears the most aerodynamic footwear ever designed . . . Beatle boots.

Thus equipped, the track racer competes in one of several different kinds of events.

1. Sprints

Match-racing, with two or three riders per race, is the most common sprint competition. Here the riders jockey for position in the early stages of the race. They do this by pedaling slowly, even standing still. They pretend they are having hot flashes or they may feign a broken leg. Then in the last 200 meters, they dash for the finish line. Points are awarded for the fastest time and the best performance in a leading role.

2. Pursuit Racing

In Individual Pursuit two riders start on opposite ends of the track and try to catch one another. The competition is enlivened if one rider has been seeing the other rider's wife.

A similar race involving two groups of four riders is called Team Pursuit. Each member of the crew takes a turn breaking wind for his teammates in order to give them a rest and sustain top speed for the

Early velodrome before the theory of banked turns was perfected.

Disc-wheel track bike.

group. The object is to catch the opposing team, establish the fastest overall time, or, if you're losing, defect to the other side.

3. Miscellaneous

The six-day race is a grueling track event sponsored by a certain manufacturer of underarm deodorant pads. These are exhausting contests in which the losers frequently beg to be shot on the spot.

The aim in the one-hour time trial is to travel as far as you can on the track in sixty minutes. It is the single most challenging event for the bicycle racer. For the spectator, however, it is much more thrilling to spend that hour watching back-to-back episodes of "Mr. Rogers' Neighborhood."

There are also many individual timed distance races such as the "Flying Kilometer" in which a heat shield is mounted on the front of the bicycle to keep it from burning up during reentry.

Road Racing

For quite a few years all bike races consisted of competitors hurling themselves around endlessly on 333-meter oval tracks. Road racing was conceived by a handful of track racers who were prone to dizziness. They were also sick of traveling to Third World countries and Shakopee, Minnesota, whenever they wanted to ride. Shakopee is a nice enough place. But if you want to have a good time there, you have to stand in line for half an hour just to ride the little mechanical pony in the Safeway parking lot. It costs a quarter for forty-five seconds and then it's back to the end of the line.

Today, road racing consists of these events.

1. Time Trial

The time trial is the race of truth. It is simply the rider against the clock. No assistance, such as drafting, coaching, or federal matching funds, is allowed. Even saying a little prayer will result in disqualification (although this practice is being challenged in the Fifth District Court of Appeals by members of a Fundamentalist sect who communicate with God by rubbing up against television sets).

The time trial may be a ten- or twenty-five-mile out-and-back course or it may be a hill climb of one to ten miles. A proper effort in the time trial should end with the rider seeking donations for an emergency heart-lung transplant.

2. Criterium

This is a race which consists, on average, of fifty laps around a one-mile circuit of city streets. With scores of riders bunched together in tight turns, accidents occur and tempers erupt. It can be a filthy, cutthroat, seamy, underhanded affair, particularly if it's done properly.

The criterium is a wonderful format for spectators who can shout encouragement to their favorites every few minutes and pelt the rest of the field with dumpster items.

3. Cross Country

The classic road race, cross country is a long-distance, point-to-point competition over farmland, desert, mountains, rolling hills, glaciers, or wherever the local domesticated bovines live.

Unless you hire a helicopter, cross country is not a great spectator sport. You may get up early, drive forty-five miles to a strategic spot, sit and wait for four hours and then, *whoooosh,* all the competitors fly by in three seconds. Wow. Big Deal. No wonder none of the major brewing companies are investing megabucks in ads that feature the superstars of bike racing. Who'd recognize them?

4. Stage Race

Cycling's ultimate test is the tour or stage race, a multiday event that combines all of the forms of road racing. One day there will be a time trial, the next day a cross-country race, the following day a criterium, and then a high-wire act.

The Tour de France is the most prestigious stage race on earth. It usually takes place in France and was the brainchild of Napoleon Bonaparte, who also worked out the theory of Neapolitan ice cream in longhand.

The leader, after each stage of the Tour de France, wears the coveted yellow jersey. Why it is coveted is perplexing. The jersey has been passed from one perspiring person to another for nearly seven hundred years without a proper cleaning. There is no time for laundromat stops in a major stage race.

Other famous stage races are the Coors Classic, Giro d'Italia, Vuelta a España, the Indianapolis 500, and the Fortune 500.

5. The Three-legged Race

Pairs of riders compete against one another in the three-legged race. Teammates station themselves side by side in such a way that their inside legs can be bound together. During the race, which may be up to one hundred kilometers long, the pair ride next to each

The three-legged race.

other, pedaling at exactly the same cadence. A team whose gear clusters are not identical will find itself in deep trouble after about three revolutions of the pedals.

This event is exceedingly popular in one or two counties in northern Nebraska where the second most popular sport is synchronized sitting. The three-legged race has failed to catch on elsewhere.

6. Citizens' Race

A citizens' race is a little get-together among a few people who happen to own bicycles. Someone marks out a course, they have a race, and the local paper boy wins. He tries to capitalize on his victory by moving to California and getting a movie contract. It never works. He's too embarrassed to return home, so he stays in Los Angeles working as a swimming-pool attendant and experimenting with drugs. He moves in with a hairstylist from Laguna Beach who is writing a screenplay and stays up past 2 A.M. on weekdays. One day his stereo gets ripped off, he loses his job, and his face breaks out.

The citizens' race should be made illegal.

Governing Bodies

Road racing is regulated by the Consumer Product Safety Commission, the National Institute for Seat Post Research, the FCC, the FAA, the Symbionese Liberation Army, the Chicago Bears, the Federal Brake Pad Board, the Boy Scouts of America, and Dick Clark.

These governing bodies are duly authorized to stuff your desk drawers with papers that look too important to throw away. Bylaws also empower them to peer in your windows at night and take notes.

To ride in sanctioned events you must complete the following form and send twelve dollars to each of the above organizations.

Once you are an official racer you will be assigned a category based on your age and your abilities. The common designations are Midgets, Intermediates, Juniors, Seniors (Category 1 or Cat 1, Cat 2, Cat 3, Cat 4), Veterans, Masters, Grand Masters, and Geezers. You move from one level to the next by improving or getting old.

If you are good enough you may eventually become a professional bike racer. Pro racers join teams that are sponsored by companies

APPLICATION FOR BICYCLE RACING LICENSE

NAME _____ EXPLAIN _____
ADDRESS _____ ZIP ___ NEAREST VELODROME ____
HELMET SIZE _____

FINGERPRINT

OFFICE MACHINES YOU CAN OPERATE:

LIST ALL COLLEGES YOU HAVE NOT HAD TIME TO ATTEND
DUE TO BICYCLE TRAINING:

DO NOT WRITE IN THIS SPACE

ARE YOU NOW OR HAVE YOU EVER
BEEN A MEMBER OF AN ORGANIZATION
WHICH ADVOCATES THE OVERTHROW OF
THE AMERICAN GEARHEAD ASSOCIATION?
☐ YES ☐ NO ☐ I CAN'T RECALL

DESCRIBE ALL DISTINGUISHING ROAD RASH DESIGNS:

WORK HISTORY:___ GENEALOGY:___ PERSONAL PHILOSOPHY:__
DOES THE NAME EDDY MERCKX MEAN ANYTHING TO YOU?__
I SHAVE MY LEGS WITH:
☐ TRAK-TWO ☐ ATRA ☐ NAIR ☐ BOWIE KNIFE
PLEASE STAPLE A URINE SAMPLE IN A ZIP-LOCK BAGGIE HERE ➡

STOP. DO NOT TURN THE PAGE UNTIL YOU ARE TOLD.

whose products are closely associated with athletic endeavors. For
example, the top teams in America are supported by convenience
store chains, alcoholic-beverage manufacturers, and the Mafia.

TRAINING

Diet

Training begins with diet. Food becomes the fuel which powers
your body and the bicycle. For best performance you should settle

for nothing but the highest-grade fuels available such as eighty-octane french fries or bite-size rocket propellant.

Some believe that riding 150 miles a day entitles them to eat enormous quantities of anything they want—chocolate chip cookies, for instance. This notion is absolutely false. Think of the grease spots chocolate chips leave on wax paper. Eat more than three a week and you'll slide off your saddle.

Develop good eating habits by following these simple nutritional guidelines:

1. Every meal should include at least one member of the four basic food groups: Hot, Cold, Lukewarm, and Munchies.

2. Everything you eat eventually comes out the pores of your skin in the form of perspiration and sticks to your jersey. Remember this fact the next time you barbecue a camel.

3. Each day eat a pound of vitamins and minerals such as limestone or chrome-molybdenum.

4. Don't talk with your mouth full.

5. Granola bars are a health-food hoax. They are leftover chunks of particle board that made one unscrupulous carpenter obscenely rich. They have no nutritional value except as roughage.

6. Green, leafy plants are good for you because, through the process of photosynthesis, they combine water and carbon dioxide, in the presence of sunlight, to form ladybugs, which are high in protein.

7. A balanced diet means that one cuisine should be offset by another. If lunch was Mexican food then dinner should be French or Italian. This rule applies only to American cyclists. Mexican, French, and Italian riders die a horrible death if they try to eat anything other than their official national meal.

8. Clean your plate. Think of the poor, starving people under contract to modeling agencies.

Personal Habits

Personal habits are as important as diet for the serious bicycle racer. It does no good to eat well and train hard during the day if you spend your nights as the kingpin in a car-theft ring.

Common sense should prevail here.

Keep your fingernails clipped, your teeth flossed, and your hair parted on the left. Never wash your whites with your colored clothes. Get eight hours sleep a night and gargle often. Use Roy Rogers or Dale Evans as a role model.

If you believe that there is a Supreme Being, know that it is His will that your faith and abilities be used to defeat and demoralize other cyclists so that they give up racing and live in cardboard boxes next to heating grates.

Call home frequently.

Training Programs

The key to good racing is good training. The first step here is to determine your present level of conditioning. An easy way to do this is to situate yourself in front of a speeding tractor-trailer rig and ride as hard as you can to stay in front. When you begin to experience brain decomposition, pull over and let the truck pass. If you are able to pedal continuously for an hour or two before suffering any ill effects, you are basically fit. If you are run over after twelve seconds, consider yourself a beginner.

Your training schedule should reflect your current physical capabilities. Below are two sample weekly programs. Feel free to modify them to meet your personal needs.

Beginning Program.

Monday. Pump up your tires.

Tuesday. Rest.

Wednesday. Get a massage. Work out the kinks in those sore muscles.

Thursday. Spin easily for thirty minutes. Then try it on a bicycle.

Friday. Hoist a few beers.

Saturday. Talk about biking for fifteen minutes. Catch a movie.

Sunday. Unwind.

Advanced Program.

Monday. Ride to Albuquerque.

Monday (later). Ride to New Brunswick.

Tuesday. Pedal uphill for nine hours, accomplished by climbing

Determine your level of conditioning by racing a semi.

Mount McKinley once or by doing sixteen million repeats on a speed bump.

Wednesday. Get a massage. But make sure it involves a jackhammer and leather items.

Thursday. Intervals. Find the center line on the roadway. Sprint the white dashes; spin easily on the blanks. Do this for the entire Interstate Highway System.

Friday. Weight training. Hoist a few beer trucks.

Saturday. Race across America.

Sunday. Unwind (for twelve minutes). Then go for a ride in a blender.

Winter Training

Winter is clearly not the best time to train on a bicycle. But in order to be competitive during the racing season, it is necessary to keep your pulse rate between 140 and 160 beats per minute from November through March.

There are several ways to maintain cardiovascular fitness when the roads are too icy for cycling. You can ride indoors on rollers which allow you to pedal your bike while watching informative public television programs such as "Washington Week in Review" or "Julia Child Stains Her Kitchen."

Similar to rollers is the Wind Load Trainer. Place your bicycle, with the front wheel removed, on a stationary frame in such a way that the rear wheel rests against a metal spindle. The spindle is attached to a cylindrical cage that defies rotation because of the air resistance of the cage and because it was manufactured in Detroit. Mount your bike. The faster you turn the pedals the more difficult it is to sustain your cadence. The Wind Load Trainer is supposed to simulate the effect of riding outdoors where wind resistance is a factor. It is only partially successful in this respect.

Whereas there is a certain training effect similar to riding into the wind, there is no cooling breeze accompanying the effort. The result is that the rider perspires so profusely that he soaks the carpet, weakens the floor of his living quarters, and severely depreciates the value of his property. Houses have been known to collapse upon a serious cyclist in the midst of an indoor workout.

Wind Load Trainer made from rollers and a politician.

Riders who own rollers may convert them to Wind Load Trainers by bolting a candidate for county commissioner about two feet in front of the rollers during an election year.

Participating in other winter sports helps keep the body tuned and prepared for spring cycling. Highly recommended are skiing, ice skating, and illicit affairs. Watching horror flicks can elevate your heart rate as can an extended conversation with an answering machine.

Some racers insist on riding their bikes in even the most inclement weather. They are the ones whose eyes are permanently frozen open.

If you want to continue riding in the winter, be prepared. Dress in layers, preferably in Fort Lauderdale. Stick your gloves in the toaster. Mount a snowplow on your front fork. Keep warm by having a heated exchange with a motorist. Get steamed over foreign policy. Carry a cask of brandy around your neck. Draft behind a Sherpa. Heed avalanche warnings.

Race Tactics

Bicycle racing is certainly a very physical sport. But it is also a complex thinking game like chess. In fact the only difference between the two sports is that in chess you don't get your bones broken unless you are a member of the Soviet national team and you botch your endgame.

There are hundreds of gambits and stratagems employed by bicycle racers. Most of these can be boiled down to four basic tactics:

Shaving Your Legs

If there was but one rule for you to remember concerning bicycle racing, let it be this one: SHAVE YOUR LEGS. Here's why.

1. Wind-tunnel tests have proven that there is an aerodynamic advantage to riding with shaved legs. The results of the testing show that over the course of a hypothetical 100,000-mile time trial, the rider who shaves his legs will beat his furry opponent by up to a nanosecond 52 percent of the time.

These results are accurate to within plus or minus 47 percent.

2. Hairy-legged riders who scrape their knees in a fall invariably develop festering sores that lead to an agonizing demise or a funny walk.

3. Shaving your legs facilitates massage. Masseurs who work on hairy racers must spend many additional hours untying all the little knots they created during the massage. In particularly snarly cases, entire Boy Scout troops have been called in to consult on the task.

4. Leg hair is the cause of static electricity in over-the-calf socks.

Clearly, then, it is beneficial to shave your legs. While you are at it, shave your eyebrows.

Breaks and Surges

You may be an extremely fit rider, but unless you have developed the skills to break away or surge during a race, you might as well give up and try a less demanding sport like humming.

You must train yourself to ignore throbbing quads and screaming bronchial tubes. Practice this routine: Ride hard at, say, twenty-eight miles per hour, then accelerate to the point where your core temperature matches that of deep-fried chicken. You'll find that it is impossible to maintain this velocity for more than a few seconds. Although there are a handful of extraordinary racers who can sustain such speeds for up to a minute, that kind of power is useless for bicycle racing. When these riders slow down, the earth has aged eight or ten years in accordance with relativity theory, and the race is ancient history.

Learn when to surge. Make your break when the other racers least expect it. Your best weapon is the element of surprise, which is chemically identical to the element carbon. Carbon, by the way, is the main ingredient in picnic barbecue fare. Eat outdoors often.

Drafting

Since it takes only an 80 percent effort to follow closely behind a rider who is expending 100 percent of his energy to maintain a certain pace, it makes sense to follow, that is *draft,* most of the race. The exception, of course, is at the finish line. Here, the idea is to jump past the leader, thank him for his contribution, and sprint in a winner. You don't make friends this way, but then this is a bicycle race, not a sorority mixer.

Conversely, if you are leading in a race, you want to discourage competitors from tagging closely behind for extended periods of time. It is easy to accomplish this task by simply avoiding personal contact with soap for about a decade.

Team Effort

In professional competition you can't win a major stage race without the help and friendship of your teammates. (Ask former champion Bernard Hinault and his bosom buddy, Greg LeMond.)

Here are a couple of situations in which teamwork may determine the outcome of a race.

Suppose you are the strongest member of your team and you have broken from the pack. To protect your lead your teammates will move in front of the pursuing riders, slow the pace down, and block

Foolproof drafting.

your opponents from passing. Your teammates can hold the pack at bay in many different ways. One of your cohorts may brandish his water bottle and scream maniacally, "Don't come near me, this is nitroglycerin!" Another of your pals can fake an attack of a highly contagious social disease which is transmitted through casual conversation. Or your teammates can lead all the riders off course and into a box canyon or a parking garage.

Teammates can help put you in an ideal spot for the sprint to the finish line. A kilometer before the end of the race they will form a pace line with you at the end. Each rider will take one turn at the front, making a superhuman effort to pull you along. One at a time they will peel off, weave to the side of the road, and spit out chunks of lung tissue. If all goes well you will be alone and rested with two hundred meters to go. At that point you had better win or else your teammates will track you down and inflate you to 150 psi with a hand pump.

World bicycle records are listed in the next section. They include track racing standards, road racing results, and a few other events which defy categorization.

THE RECORD BOOK

Former drum major Armand Vanderpool, twenty-eight, ate a Nishiki twelve-speed in one sitting. The record attempt was not without incident, however, as a brake pad lodged in Mr. Vanderpool's windpipe. A passing dwarf from Murmansk administered CPR and was credited with an assist.

The heaviest load ever carried on a bicycle: Honey Branson, thirteen, of Springbok, Connecticut, strapped a beached sperm whale on her BMX and pedaled seven miles to the nearest veterinarian's office. The whale was dead on arrival and 14,000 cans of air freshener were required before the waiting room was once again habitable.

The oldest living and active cyclist is 109-year-old Matsumito Hirokawa, an exotic dancer and part-time vitamin tycoon, whose father died in childbirth.

On April 14, 1973, Frank X. Yanker of Racine, Wisconsin, was struck by lightning four times in one day on a trip to Madison. His injuries were minor. To this day, however, he is permanently bonded to his bicycle frame.

The first American bicycle fatality occurred in Tampa, Florida, in November 1889. Dr. Amos Duffin, forty-two, tried to outrace a circus train. The train derailed and Dr. Duffin was crushed by an elephant.

Patsy Warner-Booth is the only person ever to attempt to ride a touring bike over Niagara Falls. Patsy lived for three weeks afterward but was unable to name the capital of New York when questioned by authorities.

Honey Branson tries to save a beached sperm whale.

Filbus Strang and his wife, both forty-four, and their three school-age children have lived for nearly four years on the back of a rusty Huffy dirt bike in a landfill within sight of the Statue of Liberty.

The gross national product of Tonga is $1,490.00, which is also the cost of a decent touring bike.

By 1984 bicycles existed in every nation on earth. Except Tonga.

The bicycle barrel-jumping record stands at nineteen barrels. The seven people who share this mark are all brothers from Grand Island, Nebraska. An eighth brother who won the Nobel Prize for Physics four years in a row, managed only fifteen barrels and is an embarrassment to his family.

The world bicycle altitude record was set by Tensing Noontang, a thirty-one-year-old Sherpa who reached the summit of Mount Everest in fourteen days, six hours, twenty-two minutes. Noontang also eclipsed the world land speed record in the descent by reaching Kathmandu in a shade under three minutes.

Captain George Borgias, of the Dutch Royal Air Force, rode a track bike nonstop for 162 days at a velodrome outside of Belgrade in the fall of 1983. Several weeks later he was discharged from active duty for his refusal to carry the digit 9 in simple addition problems.

Chapter 9

Maintenance and Repair

If you are like most bicycle owners when something goes wrong with your machine you probably think you can fix it yourself. DON'T TRY IT. Complete hospital wings are filled with would-be bike mechanics who were maimed in "easy-repair" accidents.

Bicycle tires are under pressure, tubing is bent against its will, exotic chemical mixtures are used in the frame. If you turn one bolt a half-twist the wrong way, the bike is liable to blow up in your face. For even the most trivial bicycle problem, leave the immediate vicinity at a brisk pace, then call The Unexploded Bicycle Squad, 1-800-321-BANG. (See below for an alternative approach to repair and maintenance.)

Some of you will not be deterred. For those of you who insist on maintaining and repairing your own bicycles, please read the following statement, sign and date it, and mail it to the publisher of this book before reading the rest of this chapter.

> Being of sound mind, and being legally bound for myself, my heirs, executors, and administrators, I do hereby release and discharge the author and publisher of *The Ten Speed Commandments* from any and all liability arising from injury while dinking around with my bicycle. I also understand the cost of this book is nonrefundable.

Signature:
Date:

The Fundamentalist approach to bicycle repair.

Tools

In addition to the tools you carry on tour, you will need these items for routine repair: pliers, complete sets of metric and standard wrenches, hammer, vise grip, posthole digger, and wheelbarrow. Store them under your bicycle seat.

Later, as you become more skilled, you will want to expand your tool set to include a road-grader and Mr. Goodwrench.

Preventive Care

You can avoid a lot of trouble if you keep your bicycle in the same condition it was when you bought it. Writers of bicycle-repair books

have discovered the best way to do this. They don't ride their bicycles. Try it yourself. Buy an expensive touring bike. Put it in a
safety deposit box for a year. Then, when you remove it, note that
there is very little tire wear, no scratches, and you have no disfig-
uring scars on your legs, elbows, or shoulders. What more could you
want?

If you insist on actually exposing your bike to sunlight and sub-
jecting it to the strain of bearing a rider, here are a few preventive
maintenance tips:

1. Rotate your tires every 15,000 miles. This practice ensures
even wear on the tire tread. It also means that half the time your
chain runs up to the front wheel. But so what?

2. Lubricate everything. Oil your toe clips, butter your brakes,
grease your saddle.

3. During winter months fill your water bottle with antifreeze.

Common Problems and How to Resolve Them

A. Flat Tire

When captive air molecules get sick and tired of serving their
sentence inside a rubber tube they get their friends to smuggle in tiny
hacksaw blades and they make a break for it. The result is a flat tire.
Repair is straightforward and logical. You'll notice that a punctured
tire is flat on the bottom, where it meets the road. In other words, the
wheel is not round. Use your hammer to adjust the spokes until your
wheel is round again. It's as simple as that!

B. Brakes Don't Work

A flat tire is obvious even when the bike is resting, unused, in the
corner of your garage. Brake problems, on the other hand, don't
become apparent until you need to use the brakes.

You may be riding down a mountain highway, approaching a
busy intersection where the light has suddenly turned red, or a cute
little cocker spaniel pup may have dashed in front of your wheel
when you discover that your brakes have failed.

In the case of the dog your reaction is clear. Go ahead and hit
him. The impact will slow you down; the fact that he's a puppy

means that you will probably not lose your balance; and something
has to be done about the plague of cocker spaniels in this country.

In the case of the mountain descent or the busy intersection, you
have no choice but to make an emergency repair. Rummage around
in your seat bag and find replacement pads for your brakes. Loosen
the retaining nuts on your brake arms and place them between your
teeth, dispose of the old pads in a fashion consistent with local litter
ordinances, substitute the new pads, and replace the nuts, assuming
you haven't swallowed them. If that does not correct the problem,
then try adjusting the cable length with a quarter-inch drill bit or a
metronome. Since you are traveling at, perhaps, forty-eight miles per
hour at this time, you should try to complete the repair in about
three tenths of a second.

C. Funny Noises

If, while riding, you find yourself bursting into laughter for no
apparent reason, most likely your bike is emitting funny noises.
"Dingalingalingalingaling" is a funny noise. So is "Bippitybippi-

Funny noises from your bicycle.

tybip." "KaBOOM," on the other hand, is a serious noise most often associated with a blown-out tire or incoming rifle grenades. All human beings take "KaBOOM" seriously. At the sound of a "KaBOOM," it is instinctive to drop whatever you are doing and seek a foxhole.

When you hear "KaBOOM" from your bicycle, you dismount immediately and trace the trouble. "Plinketyplinkplunk" doesn't cause you as much concern though, does it? If your bike says "Plinketyplinkplunk," you keep pedaling, chuckle at the noise, and plan to have a mechanic look at it next June. That attitude is dangerous!

FUNNY NOISES CAN KILL! The above example illustrates the point. "Plinketyplinkplunk" just happens to be the sound a chain makes seconds before it seizes up and pitches the rider into an oncoming recreational vehicle.

Take funny noises seriously. Listed below are some of the most familiar sounds and their origins.

Funny Noise	What It Means
Boing	You are rebounding from a collision with a fat boy on a skateboard.
Twang	Broken spoke.
Dink	You've run over a rusty Mondale-Ferraro campaign button somewhere near Minneapolis.
Wishwishwish	You have a small mammal stuck in your derailleur.

Repair Guidelines

1. Be vigilant when you overhaul your bike. Bicycles contain little metal spheres called "ball bearings." As soon as you liberate them from the bottom bracket or hubs they make a beeline for your garage drain. They travel through your plumbing, into the sewers, and eventually reach the sea where they form great reefs and major island chains.

2. Getting a sew-up tire aligned and mounted properly is harder than folding a contour sheet.

3. Eliminate annoying chain rattle by turning up the volume on your Sony Walkman.

4. If you've tried everything imaginable yet have failed to repair your bike, it is possible that your machine is possessed by evil spirits. Burn it at midnight, under a full moon, then bury the remains in Buffalo, New York.

5. Some flats will heal themselves. Put them in a closet for a few weeks and they'll be good as new except for some scar tissue.

6. If there is an unusual amount of grease built up on your chain, don't remove it. You might disturb something of archaeological interest.

7. Most repairs take about twice as long as you think they will take. They take even longer if you follow the advice offered in bike-repair manuals.

8. Contrary to what you've been told, replacement parts DO exist for your particular bicycle model. They are stored in the rear of a warehouse in Rangoon, Burma. You may obtain them by submitting to an FBI background check, passing a urine test, and putting up an international security bond in the form of gold or priceless art. Delivery takes four to six lifetimes.

9. If your bicycle throws sparks, shoot it.

10. A bicycle is little more than a toy. Don't get overly concerned with the machine's mechanical shortcomings. Your time is better spent worrying about the important aspects of life, the universal issues, things like global weather patterns.

Chapter 10

Injuries

Cycling is an excellent way to improve and maintain your health. But, as in any other intense physical activity, injury is not an uncommon occurrence. You should be aware of the types of afflictions that may befall you. Try to prevent them. When you can't prevent them, know how to treat them. And when you are laid up with an ailment, learn how to milk it for all the sympathy and chocolate-coated cherries you can get.

Here is an examination of some of the most common injuries and their treatments.

1. *BOREDOM*
Boredom is caused by taking extended tours in places like Target parking lots or Nebraska. The symptoms of this affliction vary widely with the individual. Some riders yawn and sigh and roll their eyes. Others stare, open-mouthed, at Jupiter. A few cyclists will butt their heads against large boulders, then pluck their eyebrows off, hair by hair.

In the event that you are struck with boredom, sports physiologists recommend the immediate application of ice to the brain area. Elevate the frontal lobe and immobilize the injury to prevent the damage from spreading throughout the central nervous system. Try to think about exciting things. Imagine that you just won the state lottery, took the Olympic gold medal in gymnastics, and were listed as one of the ten sexiest people since the dawn of civilization.

2. *ORGAN REJECTION*

Organ rejection is a common phenomenon among competitive cyclists who have undergone knee transplants. A year or two of pushing big gears causes the knees to detonate, spewing bone shrapnel and 10-W-40 weight knee fluid. A donor is found who is either recently deceased or who has no practical use for his knees. A quick surgical transfer of the joints is performed and the bicycle racer is back in business.

But then the trouble begins. If the body decides that the transplanted knees just don't mingle well with the other organs, it will subtly ostracize the new joints. For example, the next time the brain and muscles get together and decide to walk across the street, they won't tell the knees. The result, of course, is a fall in which the nose is broken. The nose doesn't appreciate this, but then that's the down side of classic organ rejection.

The only solution to this medical condition is the implantation of a mechanical knee. These are available through catalog sales at your neighborhood Sears Roebuck store, or, if you are handy, you can piece one together from old Volkswagen parts.

3. *CAULIFLOWER DERRIÈRE*

A poor-fitting bicycle saddle can lead to an agonizing disfigurement called Cauliflower Derrière. Short of outright surgical removal there is not much that can be done about it. You can alleviate the pain somewhat by disposing of all the chairs in your house and sleeping like a horse.

4. *ROAD RASH*

Road rash is a skin abrasion that occurs when you skid across the asphalt after a crash. It is one of a class of ailments which, if caught in the early stages, can be minimized.

Recognizing the early stages of road rash means realizing that in less than a tenth of a second you are going to hit the pavement and distribute the first five layers of your skin over a thirty-five-square-foot stretch of highway. Normally a tenth of a second is not much time for serious planning. But if you've ever been in a bike accident

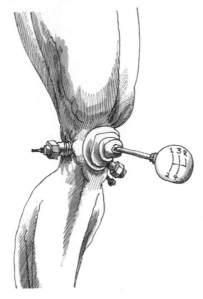

Artificial knee made from old VW parts.

you know that time suddenly downshifts into slow motion. As you plummet toward the roadway you notice every pebble on its surface, you hear the birds sing and you can pick out individual riffs and harmonies, you remember in detail an incident from childhood when your sister clubbed you over the head with a toy howitzer, then stomped on your fingers just before you passed out.

Instead of using this gift of time extension for reverie, though, you should be preparing for your imminent impact. First of all, relax. If you stiffen up, your wreck won't look spectacular. Think of Evel Knievel, the retired motorcycle daredevil. He knew how to fall. Like a graceful rag doll, he would spin and cartwheel for a full city block after failing in his attempt to leap forty school buses on a Harley. TV reporters would rush over and prop him up with a cameraman's tripod and Evel would grant them a smiling interview. That's class.

Model your spill after one of Evel's. While you are at it see if you can beat Evel's record of breaking 327 bones in a single fall.

Next, as you are inches away from road smack, compose and

rehearse the story of your accident. According to the charter of the American Gearhead Association (not to be confused with the Association of American Gearheads) you are allowed 75 degrees' latitude in stretching the truth. In other words, you may exaggerate and dramatize the incident to a point just this side of legendary.

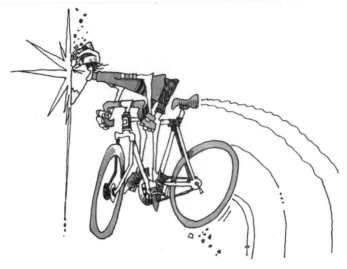

Road smack.

Finally, as a portion of your body begins to make contact with the road surface, remove and deflate one of your tire tubes, wrap it around the appropriate body part, then twist it tight with your frame pump. This makeshift tourniquet will prevent excessive loss of blood and it gives you something to do with your hands during those last boring milliseconds of your crash.

5. *GORP GAGGING*

Eating anything from a store that prides itself on its sprouts is a necessary, but often dangerous, practice for bike riders. Quick energy food from health shops is easy to carry on a tour or in a bicycle race. But gorp and granola tend to stick in your throat. Choking on a peanut or raisin is known in bike circles as "gorp gagging."

Acute compression, a common injury caused by a head-on collision with a massive object such as a mountain.

If you are a chronic gorp gagger, always ride with someone who has a graduate degree in the Heimlich Maneuver.

There are a few less common bicycle injuries worth noting. Knife wounds, midlife crisis, and the heartbreak of psoriasis are rare, but they do crop up from time to time. These and many other minor impairments can be treated through a simple program involving aspirin, whirlpool baths, and a year at Bethesda Naval Hospital.

Chapter 11

What if Cycling Is Not for You

Perhaps after reading this book, buying a bike, and putting a few miles on it, you have discovered that cycling is not your sport. If you can live with this ghastly secret, fine.

But don't do anything drastic like give your bicycle to an impoverished child. Keep it. There are practical uses for an unridden bike. Mount it on your car as a hood ornament. Turn it into a wine rack. Drill holes in it and play it like a flute. Use it as a bookmark. Wire it to your television for better reception. Plant it in your garden. Wield it as a bludgeon. Trade it for what's behind curtain Number 3.

Use an unwanted bike as a hood ornament.

LETTERS

Dear Professor Ten-Speed,

I've read loads of articles and books about exotic bicycle equipment, rigorous training programs, race tactics, expensive tours, and serious bicycle organizations. Isn't there a place in the world of cycling for some innocent fun? Can't a family just enjoy pedaling around the block with kids in tow, waving at the neighbors, maybe picking up a half gallon of milk at the grocery store? Isn't it okay to simply goof around on a bike?

Dan Avocet
Joplin, Missouri

Dear Dan,

No.

Dear Professor Ten-Speed,

I just spent $750 on an elegant dusty rose nylon-Lycra triple-layer tights-and-jacket ensemble with contrasting but complementary gloves, cap, and thermal shoe covers. What do I do now?

Sincerely,
J.S.
Wilmington, Delaware

Dear J.S.,

Go out and sweat in them.

Dear Professor Ten-Speed,

I subscribe to seven different cycling magazines, I love to spend my evenings cleaning out the notches on the bottom of my cleats with a Roosevelt dime, at any given time I can tell you within a quarter pound the pressure to which my tires are inflated, and I spend 80 percent of my annual income on cycling-related paraphernalia. Would you consider me a serious cyclist?

Buzz Gypsum
West Helena, Arkansas

Dear Buzz,
   Get serious.

Dear Professor Ten-Speed,
   I'd like to take up bicycling and perhaps win the Tour de France next year. Can you offer some advice?

Arnie Boodle
East Monroe, Louisiana

Dear Arnie,
   Yes. Get in touch with Buzz Gypsum of West Helena, Arkansas.

Dear Professor Ten-Speed,
   I'm in the market for a top-of-the-line racing bike capable of eluding enemy radar yet substantial enough to deliver a forty-megaton thermonuclear device to within six feet of a designated target. I'm willing to invest forty jillion dollars in its development with an automatic 200 percent cost overrun provision if such a machine can be built. Can you recommend a contractor?

Yours truly,
Caspar Weinberger
Washington, D.C.

Dear Cap,
   Funny you should write. Just the other day I was kicking around a very similar idea. Can we have lunch?

Dear Professor Ten-Speed,
   I recently bought my first set of sew-up tires. I thought mounting them would be easy but it has turned into one heck of a mess, I want to tell you. I've got glue all over the place and I've been stuck to the garage floor since August. Please advise.

Marilyn Overbite

Dear Marilyn,
    Stick to clinchers.

Confidential to "Perplexed in Pittsburgh":
    I've consulted with several noted medical specialists and they all agree that the disease you describe cannot be contracted on a bicycle seat as your boyfriend claims.

Dear Professor Ten-Speed,
    This is your final notice. Unless we receive payment in full on your account by the fifth of this month we will have no choice but to discontinue your telephone service.

Dear Professor Ten-Speed,
    You know what bothers me? Plastic water bottles. You ever notice in a bicycle race how one rider will take a drink and pass the bottle to another rider. Is that sanitary? And those nipples that you have to pull open with your teeth. You'd think somebody would have thought of a better way to open a water bottle. Why not just stick a straw in it? Too easy, I guess. Another thing. Why haven't they figured a way to keep liquid cool in one of those bottles? You ride twenty miles, take a drink, and it tastes like bath water.
Andy Rooney
CBS

Dear Professor Ten-Speed,
    Is Alexi Grewal the John McEnroe of bicycling or what?
Lieutenant Bilbo Glubork
U.S. Army (ret.)

Dear Lieutenant Glubork,
    Yes.

Dear Professor Ten-Speed,
    I read with interest your reply to a letter from Lieutenant Bilbo Glubork, U.S. Army (ret.). How would you like a Zefal pump inserted in your nose sideways?
Alexi Grewal

Dear Mr. Grewal,

You must have me confused with Professor Ten-Speed, the noted bicycle advice columnist.

Sincerely yours,
Professor Nine-Speed
Inventor of the digital kazoo

Dear Professor Ten-Speed,

If I travel twenty miles at 90 rpms in top gear (assuming a standard touring freewheel arrangement) over a course which drops 750 feet in elevation and a second rider begins fifteen minutes before me spinning at 75 rpms in the next lower gear, how long will it take me to overtake him if I stop once to give directions to a family of four who are trying to find an open house advertised at $159,900 with an assumable 6 percent mortgage?

Bob Lips

Dear Bob,

6 percent! Where?

Dear Professor Ten-Speed,

Is it CONNIE Carpenter Phinney, Connie CARPENTER Phinney, or Connie Carpenter PHINNEY?

Sincerely,
Connie Carpenter Phinney

Dear Connie,

Frankly, I'm stumped on this one. Can any of our readers help?

Dear Professor Ten-Speed,

Whenever I'm hosting a party I like to get the ball rolling by reciting from my bicycle training log. Everybody seems to perk up for an instant, then they all suddenly remember that they have some ironing to do at home. My question is this: Whatever happened to stay-pressed clothing?

Sincerely,
Clovis Stork

Dear Clove,

Are you familiar with the phrase, "Three teeth short of a full gear sprocket"?

Dear Professor Ten-Speed,

Is it absolutely necessary to shave your legs for cycling? I have a hunch that it's just a fad. What do you think?

Thank you,
John Piltdown
Rifle, Colorado

Dear John,

Try this experiment: Become a world-class bike racer. Then sew your lips together. Convince six of your cycling friends to do the same. Show up at half a dozen races with your pals, then sit back and wait for the fun to begin. Within three months, 75,000 bicyclists in North America alone will have sewn their lips together. You get my drift?

SUGGESTIONS FOR FURTHER READING

WINNING THROUGH HIGHER TIRE PRESSURE by Sir Hilary Mole

JESUS IS MY TANDEM PARTNER by the Reverend Billy Bob Bill Jim Joe Jones

THE JOY OF LYCRA by Olive Slick

1001 SONGS YOU CAN WHISTLE DURING A STAGE RACE by Milton Sector

THE COMPLETE BOOK OF GEAR CLUSTERS by Arthur Nosegay

CYBICLING FOR DYSLEXICS by Robert Jr. Arno

DIFFERENT SPOKES FOR DIFFERENT FOLKS by Sly and the family Stallone

THE ALL NEW COMPLETE BOOK OF GEAR CLUSTERS by Arthur Nosegay

HOW TO TURN YOUR OLD BIKE INTO A RADAR INSTALLATION AND OTHER DO-IT-YOURSELF PROJECTS by Homer E. Pair

HOW TO KNIT A CHAIN by Edith Pearl

A CONCISE HISTORY OF THE CENTER PULL BRAKE by Barbara Toynbee

960 THINGS YOU CAN DO WITH YOUR RALEIGH IN A HURRICANE by Roy G. Biv

THE COMPLETE ATLAS OF NEWSPAPER ROUTES by Larry Mondello

THE IMPROVED AND UPDATED ALL NEW COMPLETE BOOK OF GEAR CLUSTERS by Arthur Nosegay

WHY THERE IS NO REVERSE ON A TEN-SPEED by Hunter Dorfweiller

1400 BREATHING PATTERNS FOR COMPETITIVE CYCLISTS by Tom Tugg

PRIMAL COASTING by Dr. Evelyn Evelyn Oven

WHO NEEDS GEAR CLUSTERS? by Arthur Nosegay

FOURTEEN FAMOUS UNICYCLISTS by Bambi Rambino

LIVING WITH BICYCLE ABUSE by Professors Rudi Cosine and Loretta Fizz

AN ILLUSTRATED GUIDE TO VALVE STEMS by Phil Short

LEARN TO ENJOY KNEE PAIN by Rex Patella

IACOCCA'S BIKE by Iacocca

HOW TO MAKE A FORTUNE IN THE BIKE BOOK BUSINESS by Arthur Nosegay

HOW TO CRASH A PARTY ON A MOUNTAIN BIKE by Dave Derrick

IMPRESSING WOMEN BY PERFORMING BIKE TRICKS by Dave Derrick

HANDLING REJECTION by Dave Derrick

THE DAVE DERRICK STORY by Arthur Nosegay

ABOUT THE AUTHOR

Mike Keefe is the nationally syndicated editorial cartoonist for the Denver *Post*. He won the 1986 National Headliners Award for "Consistently Outstanding Editorial Cartoons." He has two kids, no pets, one wife, an electric guitar, and 112 harmonicas. He's been an avid marathon runner, triathlete, and mountain climber. Since he turned forty, however, he mostly just sits around, lying about his high school track times.